PRAISE FOR *There I Wuz! A...*   *L*

"With his signature brand of riveting pr○○, ... ; in vivid, spellbinding color."—Tawni Waters, Author, *Beauty of the Br○...*

"When we come across an aviator with a gift for storytelling, those adventures jump off the page. Eric Auxier is such an author, and *There I Wuz!* is the book."
—Karlene Petitt, Airline Pilot; CNN Correspondent; Author, *Flight to Success*

"Like watching a slide show of the life of a pilot. You will seriously enjoy this fast-paced read."—PaxView Jeff (paxview.wordpress.com)

"Eric takes our minds on a wild ride of fun, laughter, and hair-raising flying tales. A thriller!"—Jean Denis Marcellin, Pilot, Author, *The Pilot Factor*

PRAISE FOR *THE LAST BUSH PILOTS*

"TOP 100, BREAKTHROUGH NOVELS, 2013!"—Amazon.com

"Suspense and drama in spades. Romantic entanglements and a covert mission help this aviation tale take off."—Kirkus Reviews

"You won't put it down while the midnight sun still shines!"—Airways Magazine

"A pleasurable and entertaining read!"—Online Book Club

"Eric Auxier is the next Tom Clancy of aviation."—Tawni Waters, Author, *Beauty of the Broken*; *Siren Song*; *Top Travel Writers 2010*

"I flew through *The Last Bush Pilots* in one sitting, keeping my seatbelt securely fastened!"—John Wegg, Editor, *Airways* Magazine

"The author paints pictures with words that are every bit as beautiful and moving as anything ever drawn or photographed."—Aviationguy.com

"As an Alaskan bush pilot, reading *The Last Bush Pilots* was like a glance in a mirror.—CloudDancer, Airline Pilot, Author, *CloudDancer's Alaskan Chronicles*.

PRAISE FOR CODE NAME: DODGER Young Adult Spy/Fly Thriller Series

Mission 1: Operation Rubber Soul—"Flawless execution of the plot line, with a multi-dimensional protagonist that sets this book apart from the rest. Fast paced, well choreographed action and bits of simple humor."—*Online Book Club*

"Like *Harry Potter*, this YA novel is fun for kids of all ages."—Tawni Waters, Author, *Beauty of the Broken; Siren Song; Top Travel Writers of 2010*

Mission 2: Cartel Kidnapping—"4/4 STARS! Fast-paced, action-packed, and well developed. Auxier grabs the reader. Reluctant and avid readers who enjoy teenage fast-paced spy adventures will love reading this book."—*Online Book Club*

Mission 3: Jihiadi Hijacking—"4/4 STARS! Superb on so many levels. A a well-executed juggling act with just the right amount of humor. A highly detailed, entertaining, and character-driven spy thriller!"—*Online Book Club*

"An engaging espionage tale that aims to enlighten readers!"—*Kirkus Review*

Books and Works by Eric Auxier

There I Wuz! Adventures From 3 Decades in the Sky—Volume I
There I Wuz! Adventures From 3 Decades in the Sky—Volume II
    —V. II also available on audiobook at audible.com
There I Wuz!—Volume III on Audiobook
    —Target release date, Christmas, 2016, at audible.com

The Last Bush Pilots
    —An Amazon Top 100 Breakthrough Novel, 2013
    —Also available on audiobook at audible.com

Code Name: Dodger
    A Young Adult Spy/Fly Thriller Series for Kids of All Ages
        Mission 1: Operation Rubber Soul
        Mission 2: Cartel Kidnapping
        Mission 3: Jihadi Hijacking
        Mission 4: Yakuza Dynasty

Also by Eric Auxier

Blog: Adventures of Cap'n Aux (capnaux.com)
Columnist—Airways Magazine
Columnist—AirwaysMag.com

Got eBook?

If you purchased this book in print via Amazon, get the eBook version for only $1.99! Bonus material! Color photos! Videos! Hotlinks and more!

Link: amazon.com/author/ericauxier

*A portion of author proceeds benefit the orphan charities
kinshipunited.org and flyingkites.org*

THERE I WUZ!

ADVENTURES FROM 3 DECADES IN THE SKY
VOLUME III

BY ERIC "CAP'N AUX" AUXIER

Published by EALiterary Press.

Printed in the United States of America.
ISBN-13: 978-1533064981
ISBN-10: 1533064989

THERE I WUZ!

ADVENTURES FROM 3 DECADES IN THE SKY

VOLUME III

TABLE OF CONTENTS

DEDICATION

Dedicated to Aunt Pat

Your perpetual smile and infectious giggle
are lessons to us all!

FOREWORD by Captain Richard de Crespigny

A-380 Captain, Author, QF32

Photo courtesy Richard de Crespigny

Aviation regulations are written in blood. They protect us from incidents that have taken thousands of lives of our predecessors. But that is not enough.

Professional pilots commit to a lifetime of learning. Even with thousands of hours logged in numerous aircraft types, we learn something new every time we fly. Politics change. Economics, technology and companies change. Pilot roles don't. We are the last line of defense who must keep in front of change and protect the traveling public.

The best lessons happen unexpectedly. We never know when we will next be challenged and when some tidbit of information, however small, is going to become useful to resolve an emergency or abnormal situation. So we read books, study manuals, "armchair" fly and do deliberate hard practice in simulators during annual recurrent training. We study human factors and involve ourselves in safety management systems. With years of study and practice, we hope we are prepared to expect the unexpected.

Failure is not an option. The price for failure in aviation is high. Whilst high paid medical surgeons operate on and are responsible for the life of one patient, pilots are responsible in one flight for the lives of over half a thousand. We strive to improve and learn from our own mistakes and the stories of those who flew before us. Every story contains pearls of wisdom and experience. Sometimes pilots' errors are tragic. Other times we escape with only our egos damaged. The best pilots know a tarnished ego is the cheapest price to pay on the path to resilience.

Being humble and understanding our vulnerabilities is the first step to embracing the human factors and safety culture in high tech aviation. It's also the first step to managing effective teams that save lives. The humble amongst us who give and share their knowledge and stories also grow into legends and enter folklore.

Enter Cap'n Aux.

Captain Eric Auxier is not just a pilot, he is an aviation author, ambassador and legend. He is not just one of the rare breed of passionate and expert aviators who flies the big jets, but one who opens the bullet-proof cockpit door, welcomes us in, then shows us inside the culture of the most technically advanced, risk laden, yet safest profession.

I hope you enjoy Eric's collection of stories. They will make even hardened aviators crack a smile and admit we are human. These are paving stones marking our progression through a lifetime of learning. These are insights into the minds and experiences of pilots that target perfection whilst knowing it can never be achieved.

Safe flying,

Richard de Crespigny

Captain Richard Champion de Crespigny is an A380 Captain for Qantas airlines with over 18,000 hours of flight time.

A graduate of the Royal Australian Air Force (RAAF) Academy with a Bachelor of Science–BSc (Physics and Mathematics) from Melbourne University, he has flown diverse aircraft such as the deHavilland Caribou, Iroquois helicopter, Boeing 747 and Airbus A330.

His Number 1 best-seller, QF32 (visit QF32.com), won the Indie Non-Fiction Award, Independent Booksellers, and the Non-Fiction Book of the Year 2013, Australian Book Industry Awards.

He is a worldwide sought-after speaker (TheFordhamCompany.com.au/Clients/Richard-de-Crespigny)

He has been awarded the Member in the General Division of the Order of Australia, Qantas Chairman's Diamond Award, Flight Safety Foundation Professionalism Award and the Guild of Air Pilots and Air Navigators "Hugh Gordon–Burge Memorial Award". He is a Doctor of the University (honoris causa) of Charles Sturt University. He is a patron of Disabled WinterSport Australia and a Fellow of the Royal Aeronautical Society (FRAeS).

Be sure to read Captain Richard de Crespigny's fascinating book, QF32, available at QF32.com.

PREFACE—Welcome Aboard!

Author photo courtesy tonymandarich.com

Ladies and gentlemen, welcome aboard Volume III of *There I Wuz! Adventures From 3 Decades in the Sky*!

Three decades? Did I say three decades? Lordy, it's been nearly four decades now since I took that first leap into the air in a hang glider as a daring (and perhaps foolish?) young teen. (See, *Go Jump Off a Cliff!* in Volume 1 for that story.) My, how time flies when you're, well, flying!

Many of the stories in this volume have appeared in one form or another in that wonderful aviation publication, Airways Magazine, where I write as a Columnist, and its online counterpart, AirwaysMag.com (formerly AirwaysNews.com). In addition, several have appeared on my *Adventures of Cap'n Aux* blog (capnaux.com).

While I started the blog to relay some of the wild adventures in my nearly 40-years of flying, over time, the blog has evolved. I now write about a wide array of aviation-related topics, hoping to enlighten the reader not only on life in the cockpit, but the pilot's life in general. A large section of capnaux readers are upcoming pilots, and I feel a deep sense of responsibility to educate and advise—I hope in an entertaining way—this "NextGen."

As such, this book series itself has evolved. In Volume III, you will still find plenty of *There I Wuz* adventures to titillate your "chairborne" passions, but you will also find much more.

Along with a compassion for our NextGen of pilots, so, too, have I developed a sense of responsibility to tackle some of the pervasive aviation falsehoods and abuses perpetuated by everyone from self-proclaimed "aviation expert" journalists to greedy corporate management types, and even pilots themselves—hence, the section entitled, "The Cap'n Strikes Back."

Another new section I am very proud to present is "Honoring Our Military." While I never served in uniform, several close members of my family have, such as my father, brother, uncles and nephew. Therefore, I have always striven on the blog and in other writings to honor our military heroes and veterans. In this section, you will find contributions from several military pilot-writers. Their *There I Wuz!* tales will give you a new, eye-opening and jaw-dropping perspective on our adventures in the sky. Nope, we civvie pilots most certainly do *not* have a corner on the *There I Wuz* market!

I hope you enjoyed Volumes I and II, but if you haven't caught them, don't worry. Each book in this series stands alone—as does each story in this book—with its own tales of aviation adventure, humor, heartache and fun. Feel free to skip around read them in any order you like.

Except where otherwise noted, every story in this work is true, and represents what is, for me, a literal lifetime of adventures in the sky.

Whether you are a seasoned warrior of the sky, fledgeling pilot about to embark on your own lifetime of adventures, or a certified "avgeek," I invite you to sit back, relax (well, as best you can, some of these stories are pretty hairy) and enjoy the ride.

By the way, I thought it apropos to write this Preface while cruising at an altitude of 33,000', enroute from KCLT to KPHX. But don't worry: I'm not flying this baby, but riding as a passenger in the cockpit jumpseat!

Happy Hunting,

Eric Auxier
March 1, 2016

SECTION 1: Inflight Emergency

Black Swan Event: The Captain de Crespigny Story
Originally published in Airways Magazine July/August/Sept 2015

Photo courtesy Richard de Crespigny

"Seven minutes after takeoff, engine number two exploded. The failure of the engine was not the critical problem. The problem was the loss of the systems."

This is perhaps my proudest work of 2015: a three-part interview with Richard de Crespigny, the Qantas Captain who's A380 suffered an engine explosion, damaging all but one system onboard (the O_2 system, which was not used during the emergency). In an amazing demonstration of airmanship, CRM and human ingenuity, Captain de Crespigny and crew saved the ship and its passengers, who all walked away with not a single injury. The interview here includes excerpts from all three parts.

For even more, see my three, 15-minute video interviews online as well. Search capnaux.com or AirwaysMag.com for, "Black Swan Event."

His name is Captain Richard Champion de Crespigny. He flies the world's largest passenger aircraft, the Airbus A380, for Qantas Airways.

And on November 4, 2010, on Flight QF32 from Singapore to Sydney, he and his crew suffered what is called a "Black Swan event."

A "black swan" is an event so rare as to be unpredictable, but one that comes with major consequences. For example, 9/11, Pearl Harbor, or the Black Monday financial market meltdown.

Captain de Crespigny's black swan came in the form of an engine failure.

A simple engine failure on a four-engine jet such as the A380—or even on a two-engine jet, for that matter—would not be much of an event. Moreover, it is extremely rare; only one out of every five pilots will experience one in their career.

Even so, flight crews train for engine failures all the time. So, too, hydraulic failures, electrical failures, flight control failures—you name it, the professional airline pilot has practiced it.

But how about all system failures at once? This is what Captain de Crespigny and his crew experienced when their Number 2 engine exploded inflight, resulting in a grueling, four-hour event.

Best-selling author of the award-winning book, *QF32*, Captain de Crespigny is now a worldwide sought-after speaker.

This is his story.

Cap'n Aux: Welcome aboard, Captain. Thank you for joining us. You're now a worldwide, sought-after speaker, and no doubt you have this story down. Can you tell us what happened on that fateful day?

de Crespigny: Well, it was the 4th of November 2010. We were flying from Singapore to Sydney, and seven minutes after takeoff, engine number two exploded. It was the turbine disk itself that exploded. It broke off in three pieces. Two pieces missed the airplane. One piece hit the airplane and caused some shrapnel, a bit like a cluster bomb or like a grenade. Some 500 impacts on the airplane and on the fuselage were detected. It also made some major holes in the aircraft, and it cut about 650 wires and damaged 21 out of 22 systems. *(Note: only the crew 02 system was unaffected. At the low altitude, however, the system was not needed nor used.)*

The failure of the engine was not the critical problem. The problem was the loss of the systems, so we really had to assess what we had left of the computerized aircraft and find the best way on how to get it down on the ground. That took us two hours in the air, and on the ground there was another two hours of decision-making to really guarantee the safety of the passengers as much as possible. And that was a very difficult time in terms of decision-making. And then we got the passengers off, they all got home, there were absolutely no injuries for our black swan event.

There are a lot of lessons out of all the things that we did, which is really an amalgamation of all the skills you've learned through osmosis in your flying career. I've been flying for almost 40 years now, so you learn things during that career. So, all of the decisions you make are a culmination or a result of all the knowledge that you assemble and the experience and the training, and teamwork.

Speaking of teamwork, there were five pilots in the cockpit that day, the culmination of some 150 years of experience. But you all had to put all of your heads together to get the plane down on the ground.

That's right. QF32 really is a story of teamwork. Aircraft these days are too complicated to be flown by one pilot. It's a team-based organization where you trust everyone to do their jobs, and they all did.

We had eight teams, and they all did their job. It was a great outcome. QF32 is the story of team excellence.

In your book, you mention CSM (Cabin Service Manager) Klaus Michael Von Reth. You credit him with doing a phenomenal job leading the cabin crew and dealing with the passengers. Can you elaborate on that?

The industry perhaps takes cabin crews for granted. They do a great job. As I wrote in the book, Michael Von Reth was probably more qualified to be in the cabin than I was to be the Captain of the aircraft.

The SOPs (Standard Operating Procedures) didn't cover what Michael did that day. This wasn't a standard procedure anyway; we were in a black swan event. So, we really didn't have too many procedures to work with. But Michael created procedures on the fly, he was doing things that were natural to him because of his experience and background—he'd been a member of the European Space Agency— and it all came together.

Michael led an excellent crew, and the crew kept the passengers calm, and the passengers all actually became part of the team as a consequence. Michael mustered 440 passengers into a team that actually helped us on that day. And that's part of the reason why there were no injuries. So, Michael Von Reth really deserves the highest credit for what he did on that aircraft, though he really hasn't been acknowledged. So when I do my talks around the world, I try to make sure that everyone appreciates just how important he was in his position, and what a fantastic job he did.

And obviously you were between a rock and a hard place in the landing itself, not only with the critical speed, but also determining which configuration would work best for you.

The flaps weren't damaged at all. So, we landed at Flaps Three (third setting). That's what the system came up with, I'm presuming to give us "go-around" (aborting landing, climbing out and circling around for another try) capability. But we had no leading edge slats, a little "aileron droop" to give you a lift function, and lost some of the wing's boundary layer (smooth air flow) because of all the damage to the leading edge of the wing. We had a hole in the wing that air was venting through. Also, when the ailerons don't droop, you lose lift. But our ailerons weren't even faring level with the wing. The ailerons were sticking up full-scale deflection, 18 degrees up (losing lift and causing massive drag). So, there were lots of reasons we'd lost lift, and these causes were not being taken into account by the landing program and the flight instruments, so the V_{LS} (lowest selectable airspeed) display was wrong for our aircraft, which was why we were getting speed and stall warnings on the approach. So, we had incorrect flight instrumentation, we had incorrect computer calculations.

You credit First Officer Matt Hicks for pointing out that a 146-knot approach speed was going to be too slow. Basically, he used his judgment as a pilot to overrule the computer.

Absolutely. We're dealing now with highly computerized systems, and if you don't make an effort to get to understand the core of these systems, then you might become a victim or you might think the airplane is flying you. So, if you want to go to a high-tech aircraft that is run by computers, there is a responsibility to understand the underlying systems if you want to use them. Because when those systems fail—and they do fail—it's up to the pilot now to recover an aircraft that is very complex and much more sophisticated. And we've only got two pilots these days flying the aircraft, where in the past, with simpler aircraft, we had many more pilots. But the automation now lets us have two pilots to run a very complex aircraft.

Many people said we should've just thrown the aircraft down on the ground. I disagree. We had to work out what we had left, and how we would get that down onto the ground.

So, when the automation fails, it's still the pilot's responsibility to get the passengers down on the ground. The new aircraft today, if it's not on fire, then you generally have time to sort these things out, reverse-engineer these machines and treat it just like a flying lawn mower, and work out how to get the machine down onto the ground. This takes time. And you need a sense of reasonableness.

And that's what Matt had, a sense of reasonableness to know that, when the slats didn't come out, the approach speed had to increase. So, in amongst all the stress of things going wrong and all the alarm bells going off, when he was given an approach speed that was similar to the normal approach speed, he knew instinctively it was wrong, he said that is wrong. And he was correct. And he did that sitting in his seat under high stress. And so Matt did a great job. I'm very proud of Matt.

Yes, and kudos to you, Captain, for pointing that out. In our new, enlightened CRM environment, it takes everybody to fly that airplane, and the Captain is not just God.

As you know, we have a pilot flying (PF) and a pilot monitoring (PM).

Chummin' with aviation royalty: Captain Richard and I take in the Oshkosh night airshow with Captain Sully.

And the Captain, really has to aviate, navigate and communicate. So, the Captain must work hard to stay unloaded, so that he can command the situation and be on top of it. He has to assign tasks to other people and then let them do their job—not micromanage. He's monitoring what the other pilot is doing; he's monitoring what's happening in the cabin. He has to keep a situational awareness.

The role of the Captain is really a leadership role, and it's getting the best out of your team. And that's the point. A win, in a situation like any aircraft situation, is a team win. Failures are because of the Captain, because they haven't led it.

Airways Magazine April, 2015 issue included my story entitled, "Medical Emergency," (also in "There I Wuz!—Volume 2) which emphasizes CRM and the fact that the captain has to make difficult decisions in limited time, all while traveling at eight miles a minute. But it all boils down to exactly what you said, something that students are taught from Day One: aviate, navigate, communicate.

That's right. Your job is to fly the airplane, and that was our first reaction: level the aircraft and sort out the fact that we were flying. We had the auto thrust fail. And to stabilize the aircraft, make sure we weren't going to fly into the hills to which were aimed towards. So, you aviate first, then navigate and then communicate. And so, we kept that priority the whole time.

Now, we had five pilots on the crew that day. And all five pilots were very, very busy on the flight deck. We had Matt head down, doing ECAMs [Electronic Checklists. ECAM stands for Electronic Centralized Aircraft Monitor, i.e., the computers that detect failures and present the appropriate checklists on a display screen.] I was head up, keeping a global situational awareness. I told Mark, who was the third pilot, "Mark, if Matt and I are looking down, then you look up. If we're looking up, then you look down." You should never have everybody looking at the same thing at the same time.

*There came a point when you said, "Stop. Let's invert the thinking."
Tell us about that.*

Well, the Airbus has a philosophy of providing notification of failures (via the) ECAM. The A380 has 250,000 sensors feeding in, and when there's an error, the flight warning computers look up the error message in the database and sees if there is a procedure. We have 1,225 checklists in the A380. So, it would pull up the checklist procedure to handle that particular error.

So, when we had 650 broken wires and half the network slashed, the numbers of either errors that came through, or inconsistent messages—because wires weren't just being cut, they were shorting with other wires—it created an overload of ECAM messages. ECAM was designed to make your life easy. But the ECAM, in our case, made life hard, for three reasons: One, it was an overload; there were too many. And the second reason is because some of the ECAMs were wrong, because the sensors were faulty. And if we would have followed the checklist, perhaps we wouldn't be here today. So, we were very critical and skeptical of the systems, and many checklists we actively did not do.

The third thing is that the ECAM checklist is really designed for a single point of failure.

So, we had lost 65% of our roll control, and that might be OK if we were in balance. But we had three fuel imbalances that were all out of limits.

So, the ECAM would give single errors

Nancy-Bird Walton

that we were having trouble keeping up with. So, I'd lost my mental model of where the aircraft was, and how I was going to be able to control it later on. ECAM didn't work, and I'd lost the picture. And at that point, I inverted the logic and said, "Instead of looking at what's failed, start looking at what's working."

That is a pure follow-on from Gene Kranz in the situation of Apollo 13. Gene's mission controllers in Houston were also melting down, because Apollo 13 had all these failures, and the mission controllers didn't know how to resolve it all. Gene said, "Stop wondering at what's failed, and let's focus on what's working."

And that's what we did. And that made a complex A380, with four million parts and with 1,225 checklists and 250,000 sensors. It turned it into a glorified Cessna, and at that point it became simple.

Team Aux & Capt. de Crespigny at Oshkosh 2015: L-R Cap'n Aux, Producer Bunny, Transportation Engineer Cap'n Dave, Capt. de Crespigny and wife Coral.

You spent another two hours on the ground assessing the danger. Why didn't you evacuate immediately?

This is a very complex problem. The ultimate answer is that you do whatever it takes to protect your passengers. You have standard operating procedures that work in standard situations. This was not standard. We had an engine that wouldn't shut down, we had four tons of fuel leaking near hot brakes, and we had a whole lot of other nasty situations.

To evaluate whether to chuck the passengers down the slides straight away, you have to understand the risks connected with doing so. In an evacuation, 15% of the passengers will end up in a hospital. With the exception of the 747s and 777s, all the doors on the A380 are higher than those on any other aircraft in America.

You also have to look at the flash point and flame front speed of jet fuel, at what fire and rescue services you have nearby, at all the threats outside, which are many.

One of the worst things you can do in aviation is to presume or assume. In other words, people assumed and presumed that the brakes under the wing were hot. However, we never assumed anything. We waited for signs of fire, and there probably would not have been fire, for the reasons above. We only found out six months after the incident that the brakes under the wing were cold. If we had presumed that they were hot and had evacuated, I think that there would be people who would not be here today. We didn't presume; we waited for factual evidence of fire. It didn't come, we kept them on board, we had no injuries.

It will be a different decision, on any other day, for any other crew on an aircraft. But every pilot should be armed with the knowledge to make that decision, which is a continuous process, using every bit of CRM that you can muster.

Captain Richard Champion de Crespigny is an A380 Captain for Qantas airlines with over 18,000 hours of flight time. For more information, see his Foreword in this book.

Be sure to read Captain Richard de Crespigny's fascinating book, QF32, available at QF32.com.

Oshkosh photos by Team Aux's Tech Supervisor John "Otto Pilot" Keith; all other photos courtesy of Richard de Crespigny.

The author would like to thank Elliot Hayot for his help with this piece.

Inflight Heart Attack
An Interview With AA 550 FO Steve Stackelhouse

Originally published in Airways Magazine and AirwaysMag.com,
February, 2016

Photo courtesy Steve Stackelhouse

"I declared a medical emergency with ATC and began
searching for the nearest suitable airport."

Tragically, my airline lost one of its finest last year, as my friend Captain Mike Johnston suffered a heart attack in flight.

First Officer Steve Stackelhouse, an excellent pilot with whom I've flown many times, saved the day by diverting for a safe landing.

Unfortunately, however, we still lost Captain Mike. In this exclusive interview, Steve relates the story.

It was expected to be a routine flight.

A red-eye transcon, commanded by veteran American Airlines Captain Mike Johnston and assisted by First Officer Steve Stackelhouse. Both fully qualified and type-rated Airbus pilots, they were to fly 147 passengers, two infants and crew in their A320 from KPHX (Phoenix, Arizona) to KBOS (Boston, Massachusetts).

As flight crews typically do, the two pilots planned to trade off flying each leg during their three-day trip together. The first leg would be flown by Captain Johnston.

"We were cruising at Flight Level 350 (35,000 feet,) about three hours and forty five minutes into our red-eye," said First Officer Stackelhouse. "We were still 250 miles from BOS and the sun was just starting to rise in the East."

Stackelhouse observed Johnston take a few breaths from his oxygen mask, but didn't think anything of it. A few hits of O_2 is a common way for pilots to refresh themselves, especially during red-eye flights.

"He gave me zero indications that he was in any kind of distress," Stackelhouse said. "Mike put his mask down and laid his head back. Within a minute, I heard the 'snore'—what would later be described as his final breath."

Steve and his crew receive the American Airlines Chairman Award for meritorious service. Center: Jennifer Sullivan, the flight attendant and registered nurse who helped work on Captain Johnston. On right: AA CEO Doug Parker

Thinking Johnston had fallen asleep or unconscious, Stackelhouse shook the Captain, but got no response. He immediately called Lead Flight Attendant Jennifer Sullivan, a registered nurse, who began assessing the patient. She could not find a pulse.

"She stated that we needed to land the plane *now*," Stackelhouse said. "I declared a medical emergency with ATC and began searching for the nearest suitable airport."

Normally, during an emergency, both pilots would divide duties, with one flying and handling the radios, while the other dealt with the emergency. But this time, Stackelhouse was solo.

"I went into a sort of calm, mission-oriented mode," Stackelhouse said, "to very methodically go through the process of getting on the ground quickly."

The A320 is a highly automated airliner, which greatly relieved Stackelhouse's workload. Even so, as a single pilot, during the following minutes, he was extremely busy—simultaneously flying the airplane, handling the radios and searching for an alternate.

Stackelhouse also typed the situation into the plane's ACARS, or Aircraft Communications Addressing and Reporting System, to alert his company dispatcher. On any given flight, the Captain and Dispatcher will jointly decide if and what airport is suitable for a diversion. The system is often somewhat cumbersome and slow to respond, however, and Stackelhouse received no immediate reply.

He had to decide on his own.

Stackelhouse said, "I identified KSYR (Syracuse, New York) as the closest suitable airport, even though we were about 50 miles past it, to the East. I had landed at KSYR before, so I felt somewhat familiar. I asked for direct KSYR."

ATC complied, and gave him a descent to 11,000 feet. As an emergency aircraft, flight 550 would receive priority handling.

While Stackelhouse made the high dive for Syracuse, flight attendant Sullivan worked on the patient. However, with the man firmly strapped to his seat, she was able to offer little help.

Photo courtesy Steve Stackelhouse and his lovely family.

Furthermore, pulling the Captain from his seat might risk entangling him in the airplane's controls, so it was decided that he should remain strapped into his seat.

"We were on the ground within what

seemed like a few minutes," Stackelhouse said. "It all seems so surreal now."

Steve quickly taxied to the gate. Once parked, paramedics rushed onboard.

"The paramedics did attach what appeared to be EKG leads to Mike upon landing." Stackelhouse said, "but there were no signals at all."

Captain Michael Johnston was pronounced dead.

A relief crew was flown in to take the passengers on to Boston, while Stackelhouse and the original crew were released from duty. Indeed, Stackelhouse had known Captain Johnston for some time and, afterward, was understandably shaken.

"Mike and I we were based together in KLAS (Las Vegas) years ago," Stackelhouse reminisced. "We had flown several trips together. Mike was always very friendly, and we had many a conversation."

Stackelhouse is back flying the line. But, somehow, the experience has served to strengthen his already strong ties to his family.

Together with Kris, his wife of 22 years, he continues to raise three children. His future plans include living in a lake home with his wife, and enjoying their time together traveling.

Life—and the flights—must go on.

"To fly West, my friend, is the one final check we must all take."
—Author Unknown

Stackelhouse said he often thinks of Mike and his family.

"I pray that they will find peace knowing Mike died while doing what he loved," he said.

Steve and I would like to express our deep condolences to the family and loved ones of Captain Michael Johnston.

What is a "Co-Pilot?"

One of the most annoying misnomers for us piloty-types is the misunderstanding of just what a "copilot" is. After First Officer (i.e., "Copilot") Steve Stackehouse's emergency landing (see previous story), he stated that he had been barraged by silly questions such as, "Was that your first-ever landing?" It brings to mind John Merrick's famous line in *Elephant Man*: "I am not an animal. I am a man!" Folks, *Co*-Pilots are *Pilots*. Period. Let's set this record straight once and for all . . .

"Pilot Dies Inflight; Co-pilot Makes Emergency Landing!" **trumpets one sensationalized headline.**

To hear the typical media say it, one would get the impression that disaster was narrowly averted for all on board when the "co-pilot"—gasp! —took over to fly.

One would also get the impression that airliners are flown single pilot, and that "co-pilots"—more properly referred to as First Officers—are merely hanging around to do nothing more than act as their captain's personal coffee barista. Indeed, the term "co-pilot" itself carries the implication that they are not real pilots, but sort of an apprentice pilot in training.

Nothing could be further from the truth.

"The one thing that struck me as odd throughout this entire experience," Stackelhouse said, "was that many people have very little idea about what it means to be a First Officer at a major airline in the United States."

Stackelhouse said he got comments from friends and even family that seemed to indicate there was an enormous misunderstanding concerning exactly what the First Officer, or "co-pilot," does. He wants people to know that First Officers are equally as qualified to operate the airplanes they fly as the Captain.

Every once in awhile, I'm blessed to fly with Steve on the line.
But watch out: his knight game is deadly on the chessboard!

"We receive the same training and licensure as the Captain," Stackelhouse said. "Pilots throughout this business often times joke that, as a Captain, you should treat your First Officer well—because they may be your Captain at your next airline."

Stackelhouse believes the seniority system used for promotion is partly to blame for the disconnect. At most airlines, the upgrade to Captain is based solely on seniority—that is, how long one has been at the company, relative to all other pilots.

"I had several people tell me that this event should look good on my resume and help provide a quicker promotion for me to the Captain's seat. When I explained to them that there is no such thing as performance-based promotion, their eyes would glaze over. In this business, you are only promoted to Captain when your seniority number comes up."

Indeed, the system has nothing to do with performance or experience. In fact, any pilot hired at a major U.S. airline is already qualified to be a Captain of any size plane; all that is needed is the aircraft-specific systems and procedures training for the metal to which they are assigned.

And First Officer Stackelhouse's qualifications? Over 16,000 total flight hours, including over 10,000 hours in Airbus 319/320/321 models. He has a B.S and M.S. degree from the University of North Dakota and an Airline Transport Pilot license. He is type-rated in both Beechcraft 1900 and Airbus 320 aircraft.

Now that's one highly experienced coffee barista!

SECTION 2: Lessons Learned (the Hard Way)

With Capt. Bill Palmer: Understanding AirAsia 8501

Originally published in Airways Magazine and AirwaysMag.com, April, 2016

Eric Auxier
&
Bill Palmer

COLUMNIST
Airways Magazine

"Both pilots tried to recover—one by pushing and the other pulling."

This was Captain Bill Palmer's and my second collaboration, after our piece on the MH370 mystery, written shortly after its disappearance. (See Occam's Razor and MH 370, on NYCAviation.com.) Captain Palmer's insights and knowledge continue to impress.

If you have read his book, *Understanding Air France 447*, you were no doubt struck by his depth of knowledge, exhaustive research and, most of all, his innate ability to explain an extremely complex situation to a general audience. As one reader put it, the book reads like "a thriller, a horror novel, and a technical manual, all wrapped into one."

Captain Palmer brings these qualities to our story today, as you will see.

In this piece, we analyze the findings of the investigative board from a pilot's perspective, in order to glean lessons for every aviator.

(Note: it is not our intent to point fingers, place blame, nor critique; rather, it is to learn from the issues raised.)

Aircraft accident investigations serve an important purpose: to learn what happened, so we can learn *from* what happened.

AirAsia 8501 is the Airbus A320 that crashed December 28, 2014, killing all 155 passengers and seven crew aboard. The primary investigative body, the KNKT, or Komite Nasional Keselamatan Transportasi (the Indonesian version of the US's NTSB), listed several causal factors and recommendations. While many issues such as maintenance practices were addressed in the report as well, we will only address those points relevant to pilots.

From the report:

"On 28 December 2014 an Airbus A320-216 aircraft registered as PK-AXC was cruising at 32,000 feet on a flight from Juanda Airport, Surabaya, Indonesia to Changi Airport, Singapore with total occupants of 162 persons. The Pilot in Command (PIC) acted as Pilot Monitoring (PM) and the Second in Command (SIC) acted as Pilot Flying (PF).

"The Flight Data Recorder (FDR) recorded that four master cautions activated following the failure of the Rudder Travel Limiter....The crew performed the ECAM procedure (computer resets) on the first three master caution activations. After the fourth master caution, the FDR recorded...the FAC CBs (circuit breakers) were pulled. This pilot action resulted (in).. AUTO FLT FAC 1+2 FAULT.

"Following two FAC fault, the autopilot and auto-thrust disengaged and the flight control reverted to Alternate Law...

"Subsequent flight crew action leading to inability to control the aircraft in the Alternate Law resulted in the aircraft departing from the normal flight envelope and entering prolonged stall condition that was beyond the capability of the flight crew to recover."

Several Important Explanations

—The Pilot in Command (PIC), is commonly referred to as the Captain or "pilot;" the Second in Command (SIC) is commonly referred to as the First Officer (FO) "co-pilot." In an airliner, both are fully qualified pilots and can fly the plane, but the PIC is in command. In this incident, the SIC was flying the plane. The QZ 8501 Captain, a 53-year-old Indonesian, had over 20,500 flight hours, with nearly 5,000 in type; the SIC, a 46-year-old Frenchman, had 2,247 flight hours, with almost 1,400 in type.

—FAC stands for "Flight Augmentation Computer." Among other things, the 2 FACs calculate the flight envelope and control rudder functions such as rudder travel limit, yaw damping, and rudder trim. Along with 5 other flight computers (3 SECs, or Spoilers Elevator Computers, and 2 ELACs, or Elevator Aileron Computers), the FACs aid in processing pilot and autopilot inputs.

—Rudder Travel Limiter (RTL or RTLU) is a computer which limits the swing of the rudder at high speeds, in order to prevent over-stress. The higher the airspeed, the more the travel is limited. While an important item that would need to be addressed by maintenance, the failure of the Rudder Travel Limiter should be a fairly minor issue, with little consequence if procedures are followed.

—When a Rudder Travel Limiter warning is triggered, the standard Airbus ECAM procedure (that is, the checklist that pops up on the screen) calls for resetting each FAC, one at a time, via the overhead switches. This was apparently the procedure followed for the first three failures. However, it does not call for the simultaneous resetting of both FAC computers, nor does it call for a circuit breaker reset, which was apparently what the PIC attempted after the fourth failure—a "correction" which the PIC stated he had seen maintenance personnel perform on the ground.

—On the Airbus fleet, "Normal Law" simply means the plane is fully protected against such issues as stalls and over-speeds. In "Alternate Law," these protections are removed. "Alternate Law" in itself is not unsafe; most other aircraft, such as older Boeings, do not have these protections.

So, with such minor issues, what caused a major catastrophe?

The report speculates that the SIC, the Pilot Flying, may have been distracted by the sudden failures, and spatially disoriented by the flight upset created when the autopilot kicked off:

"The rudder deflected 2°... without pilot input for 9 seconds, resulting the aircraft rolling to the left un-commanded up to 54°... The delayed response of the SIC was likely due to his attention not being directed to the PFD (*Primary Flight Display—Ed.*), as many events occurred at this time."

At the same time that the roll correction was made, a pitch-up input was also made, perhaps inadvertently, and the aircraft started to climb—with rates up to 11,000 fpm—and lose airspeed.

An initial correction was made, but not enough to return to straight and level flight:

"This rapid right rolling movement might cause an excessive roll sensation to the right. The SIC may have experienced spatial disorientation and over-corrected *while the guidance from the Flight Director was still available (emphasis added—Ed.).*"

While the report claims that the Flight Directors had been available throughout this time, this may not have entirely been the case. The Airbus manual states that Flight Directors disappear at their limits of 45° roll and +25°/-13° pitch. Once back within those limits, they will reappear. However, once they reappeared, they may have reverted to heading/vertical speed values at the time of reappearance—that is, guiding the unthinking pilot to continue in this extreme pitch attitude. (This is speculation on our part, based on the systems.) Regardless of Flight Director guidance, however, pilots are trained to fly without them. Moreover, pilots are supposed to be trained in unusual attitude upset recoveries as well, such as this scenario.

The Captain, apparently still out of his seat, then inexplicably shouted, "Pull down! Pull down!" What he apparently meant to say was, "Push down." The miscommunication seems to have been exacerbated not only by the stressful situation, but the fact that both pilots, of different nationalities, had to use English—a second language for both—to communicate.

In the confusion, the SIC continued to Pull—up. With the system degraded into Alternate Law—i.e., with no stall protections—the inevitable happened:

"The degraded performance and ambiguous commands might have decreased the SIC's situational awareness and he did not react appropriately in this complex emergency, resulting in the aircraft becoming upset..."

When the stall warning triggered, forward sidestick was only applied for a few seconds. Later, as the stall fully progressed, and the aircraft began a rapid descent, the stall warning remained on constantly, yet the FO's sidestick remained held full back.

The Captain eventually grabbed his control and pushed down. However, he did not communicate this to the SIC:

"The standard call out to take over control described in the operator SOP (Standard Operating Procedure) is, "I have control," and responded by the other pilot transferring the control by the call out, "You have control."

As a result, both pilots continued to try to recover—one by pushing and the other pulling—and therefore neutralizing each other's inputs. This would normally generate an aural "Dual Input" warning along with associated flashing lights, but the DUAL INPUT warning was suppressed by the more critical stall warning annunciation:

"...At 2317:41 UTC the aircraft reached the highest altitude of 38,500 feet and (the) largest roll angle of 104° to the left. The aircraft then lost altitude with a rate of up to 20,000 feet per minute....The last data recorded by the FDR were at 2320:35 UTC with the airspeed of 83 kts, pitch 20° up, AOA 50°, roll 8° to left, with the rate of descent of 8,400 Ft/minute at a radio altitude of 187 feet...."

Analysis

Again, Captain Palmer and I have no intention of armchair-quarterbacking this tragic accident nor the board's findings, but mean solely to glean important lessons that may be of use to pilots. To that end, we submit the following:

•In any and every situation, pilots should always "Aviate, Navigate, and Communicate." By "Aviate," we mean, first, foremost and at all times,

FLY THE PLANE. At all times, the crew must have assigned a definitive PF, or Pilot Flying.

•By far the most important lesson here is that the PF must shut out the "noise" around him—including his or her own potentially disorienting sensory inputs. Instrument students constantly have this drilled into their heads: ignore the body's sensations, keep calm and trust your instruments. In this case, however, one of those instruments may have been in error. While the report claims that "guidance from the Flight Director was still available," we believe that, during the extreme attitudes, they were not, and when reappeared may have been in error. Regardless, however, the experienced pilot must use his/her judgement to recognize that and recover using only the "raw data."

•A stall is an angle-of-attack problem and must be solved quickly by reducing the angle of attack, even if it requires pitch attitudes that are outside of normal. It is best solved at the first indication of a stall, and airline training often tends to focus on early recognition and recovery as opposed to recovery from extreme situations. Control effectiveness is understandably compromised at higher angles of attack, and beyond a certain point the ability to recover—no matter how skilled the pilot—is in doubt.

•When a failure occurs that generates a warning and checklist procedure, pilots should follow them, within reason. Just as in the case of a faulty instrument, the checklist procedure generated by the computers may be improper, so pilots must use their judgement. The crew did indeed follow the proper checklist procedures the first three times, but then deviated on the fourth, exacerbating the problem. When a reset is not successful after one or two tries, it's time to consider the item broken. The rudder travel limit system, while inoperative, did not compromise the safety or continuation of the flight.

•Pulling circuit breakers is a job for maintenance personnel on the ground, not for pilots in flight. By and large, this is a SOP strictly adhered to by most airlines. (Note: While we focus here on pilot procedures, it should be noted that the RTL had been "squawked" [written up] 23 times and never properly fixed. As the last line of defense, flight crews must put their foot down and refuse to fly such improperly-addressed maintenance.

•In a multi-pilot crew, communication is critical. This is the heart of CRM—Crew Resource Management. If, for example, a Captain wishes to take over flying duties, he must definitively state, "I have control," and the SIC must respond with, "You have control" (exact phraseology varies between airlines). This standardized communication becomes extra critical when working with crews of differing nationalities and communicating in a foreign language.

•The Captain must at all times maintain situational awareness. In the case of QZ 8501, it appears that the SIC was clearly "in the red," in Threat and Error Management (TEM) parlance. That is, he was completely overloaded to the point of not understanding what was happening, nor how to properly recover. The Captain seemed to be in the red as well, or at best "in the yellow"—overloaded, but still somewhat situationally aware.

• While both pilots appeared to be properly trained and experienced, the SIC nevertheless had fairly low time—at least relative to his US counterparts—which may have been a contributing factor. Indeed, the FAA requires a minimum of 1,500 flight hours and an ATPL (Airline Transport Pilot License) for all Part 121 (i.e., airline) operators, including First Officers. Pilots hired by a major US airline typically have several times that number. As previously stated, the 46-year-old First Officer, who was the pilot flying, had 2,247 total hours, with 1,400 of those in the A320.

In Conclusion

The Airbus philosophy is to take an extremely complex machine and task—that is, the task of flying the machine—and simplify and automate it in order to minimize distraction, and therefore maximize safety. By and large,  through its highly sophisticated systems, this works.

But, systems fail, and that is why training is critical.

Often, at the most unexpected and inconvenient times, pilots are called on to be pilots and fly the airplane under adverse conditions. An airline operation often involves using the autopilot for most of the flight, and hand-flying the airplane, especially in instrument weather conditions, is a skill that requires practice to acquire and to maintain. Over-dependence on the flight directors is a potential threat, for when the flight directors are off—or in error—the pilot must determine the proper attitude to fly him/herself.

Precisely flying the airplane with degraded flight control behaviors, unexpected roll inputs, alarms going off, and the other pilot providing contradictory orders ("Pull down") is much more difficult—for any pilot. Trying to pull that together when those skills were not well-practiced is like being told you're to give a piano recital on stage—right now, and you haven't practiced for two years.

While no airline curriculum can ever train for every possible scenario, it is crucial that simulator sessions include challenging scenarios wherein the crew must not only have a working knowledge of the airplane's systems, company SOPs and basic airmanship, but must also put their heads together to solve the problem.

Flying in unusual attitudes, with the associated unusual forces on the body, can be very disorienting. The situation is not conducive to clear thinking. Skills learned in training and practice have to take over. If those skills and abilities are not there to begin with, or are weak, the chances of success decrease.

In Summary

Pilots must always:

—Fly the Plane. All other considerations are secondary.

—Trust your instruments, unless it is obvious they are wrong. Sometimes, in a highly automated airplane, it is best to simply "turn off the magic and fly."

—Respect the stall warning (unless you have a good reason to believe it is erroneous) and reduce the angle of attack promptly.

—Follow SOPs. Studies have shown that not doing so can double errors. Also, follow checklists, but use judgement to ensure the proper one is followed.

—Don't play mechanic inflight; that's for the mechanics on the ground.

—In good weather, frequently practice autopilot/autothrust/flight director-off "raw data" flying.

—Communicate, using standard phraseology.

—At all times: Aviate, Navigate, and Communicate.

The authors wish to express our condolences to the loved ones of AirAsia 8501.

Captain Bill Palmer is currently an A330 captain and instructor pilot for a major US airline. He is type rated in A320, A330, B757/767, B777, DC10, has trained on both A350 and B787 aircraft, and is an active glider pilot. He has been teaching flying since 1978, and written numerous training materials, including major parts of several aircraft systems manuals for his employer.

Bill is also the author of "Understanding Air France 447," an in-depth exploration into the June 2009 crash of an A330. He holds a B.S. in Aeronautical Science.

Dan Pimentel: Donuts for Fisk

Pilot, Columnist, Flying *Magazine* , AOPA Pilot; *Editor,* Airplanista

Team Aux does Oshkosh!

"You can't tell airplanes to just pull off to the side of the road."

As a professional writer, general aviation pilot and one of the founding members of our Blogging in Formation team, Dan brings a unique perspective on all things aviation. Also the founder of Airplanista (airplanista.com), Dan is also known for his epic aviation meetup party called, "Oshbash," at EAA's AirVenture ("Oshkosh.")

For the week of EAA's AirVenture, better known as "Oshkosh"—the world's largest fly-in—KOSH (Whitman Regional Airport) becomes the world's busiest Control Tower. On one day at last year's event, there were more than 3,100 aircraft movements (takeoffs and landings) in 14 hours. That's an operation every 16 seconds. Over 10,000 aircraft visit the region, along with well over half a million people. KOSH is truly the annual, worldwide epicenter of aviation.

Pilot-author-blogger Dan Pimentel chimes in with this story of the unsung heroes of Oshkosh: the Air Traffic Control volunteers that safely steer said aircraft from several temporary "towers"—nothing more than a small trailers strategically placed in various fields.

Calm in the face of danger may define for us the quintessential pilot-hero, but what about a team of ATC controllers faced with an emergency, all while a flurry of aircraft buzz about their heads? As you will soon see, these smooth talkers certainly earned their wings—and donuts—this day!

(OSHKOSH, WI) A tragic accident early on day three of EAA AirVenture Oshkosh closed the airport to all arrivals and departures. The aircraft involved was a Piper Malibu with five people on board. *The Oshkosh Northwestern* reported that four people made it out before the plane caught fire; one person had to be evacuated by helicopter. We want to join the entire aviation family to keep the family of the injured in our thoughts.

Thomsen Meeks and his dad, Tom, enjoy the view at FAA's Fisk Arrival "tower" during EAA AirVenture Oshkosh. It was a perfectly sunny morning at Fisk with an upbeat vibe, until an accident at the Oshkosh air show closed the airport to incoming arrivals.

When KOSH airport closes during AirVenture, it sets up a massive chain reaction that ripples out for miles, effecting sometimes huge amounts of inbounds in the air heading to this gigantic show. Many of those arrivals fly the VFR "Fisk Arrival," which is a well-known procedure that brings all

VFR traffic over a tiny berg west of the show in a nose-to-tail "Conga Line" of all varieties of airplanes. The drill is pretty simple:

You fly at a published altitude and airspeed to Fisk, which is a temporary FAA "tower" set up to control the very high number of inbounds coming into Oshkosh. To prevent radio chatter, the controllers on the ground make a radio call based on color of plane and other features such as high or low wing, taildragger, biplane, etc. Based on type of airplane, these controllers give you a quick vector in two directions...east to make a left base to RWY 36, or down the railroad tracks to make a right downwind and base to RWY 27, with the inbound pilot instructed only to "rock your wings" as acknowledgement that they understand their assignment. It is an aerial ballet that is well-rehearsed and works very well.

What makes the Fisk arrival work so well is the high quality of the FAA controllers at the "tower," which is nothing more than an office trailer, a radio transmitter, and a giant bank of colored LED lights that flash to let inbounds ID the "tower" from the air.

Working Oshkosh each summer is a coveted assignment for these controllers, who bid for the chance to come here and work traffic during the world's largest aviation celebration.

Today I had the opportunity to join my new besties, Tom Meeks and his son, Thomsen, for a run out to visit the controllers working Fisk. We first had to swing thru the Pic N Save for donuts, because as I understand it, the "unofficial" requirement to visit is to bring donuts. They were well received, and the five controllers polished off half a dozen pastries not long after we arrived.

To get to Fisk, you head down a tiny country road, off of another country road. It sits in a non-descript field surrounded by farmhouses and grain. If not for the sea of bright pink FAA ATC shirts, this might be a cellular system work trailer, or a small construction site. You could drive right by and never know of the important work these controllers are doing. But when you stop—carrying donuts—you quickly see just how talented these controllers really are:

We were welcomed (must have been the pastries) and every controller was more than happy to explain what they were doing, and how it all worked. I was instructed to look through a dip in a grove of nearby maple trees to see a tiny speck with a landing light coming our way. That was one of a continuous line of inbounds these guys were working. This was a slow day because General Aviation (GA) parking and camping at the show was already at capacity, and still, there was a new plane every 30 seconds or so...non-stop. Two controllers ID the airplanes with binoculars, calling out the color and type. The lead controller stands and hovers around, calling out what that airplane needs to do. The last and maybe most important on the team is the radio operator, who relays the instruction via radio to the inbound. The vibe was upbeat, light, lots of joking and laughter, and it was clear these guys loved what they were doing.

Working Fisk is sort of a badge of honor for these controllers, and if you could measure their excitement level on a 10 scale, they were cruising along at a 3. Cool, calm and collected, it did not even ruffle their feathers when an unidentified plane came into view, flying southbound directly towards the inbound Conga Line. They just rolled with it, calling out the traffic. No...big...deal.

Cost of admission: While it is not officially mandated, apparently the drill is that to visit Fisk and watch some of FAA's finest controllers work the Conga Line of arrivals, there MUST be donuts involved. Photo courtesy Dan Pimentel/Airplanista.

But five minutes into our visit, the "no big deal" element changed as the crash at the show closed the airport. What that means is that Fisk now had to do something with their line of inbounds; you can't tell airplanes to just pull off to the side of the road. As the lead controller jumped on the phone to coordinate everything, the four other controllers simply started calling out holding instructions.

For airplanes outside the city of Ripon, they were sent into a hold over Green Lake, while airplanes between Ripon and Fisk were sent to hold over Rush Lake.

The controllers worked maybe 20 arrivals, shoving them into these two holds, or releasing them out of the area at pilot's request. But what was surreal was the composure of these controllers, as that needle on the excitement meter never budged. It was just another day at the office - or in this case, a trailer in a grain field - and these guys handled the closure of the airport without so much as one tiny bit of stress. That could be because they come from some of the country's busiest commercial towers, so this is just no big deal.

I have always held FAA's controllers in the highest regard; they do a tremendous job. But today at Fisk, standing five feet away from a crew working an emergency situation without one single drop of sweat made me realize that my respect for FAA's ATC team is well-earned, and truly deserved.

Dan Pimentel has worked in journalism and graphic design since 1979, and currently writes features and columns for seven national aviation magazines including Flying, AOPA Pilot, EAA Sport Aviation, HAI's Rotor Magazine, Air&Space Smithsonian, Cessna Flyer *and* Piper Flyer. *He's also the President and Creative Director of Celeste/Daniels Advertising and Design (celestedaniels.com) in Eugene, Oregon. He's an instrument-rated private pilot and owner of a 1964 Piper Cherokee 235, and has been writing the Airplanista Aviation Blog (airplanista.com) since 2005. You can find him on Twitter as @Av8rdan. Each summer at EAA AirVenture Oshkosh, he hosts the #Oshbash social media meet-up event during the show.*

Photos in this piece courtesy of the author.

Top 5 Improvements in Modern Aviation Safety
Originally published on AirwaysMag.com

"Many improvements in aviation have come off the backs of airline tragedies."

While the airline accident du jour continues to (annoyingly) grab the headlines and be overanalyzed *ad nauseum* by the media's self-proclaimed yet often clueless "experts," airline safety continues to improve by leaps and bounds. All this blathering tends to worry the public, giving them a false perspective on aviation safety.

In recent decades, however, improvements and inventions have transformed the cockpit—and thus the airline industry—from impressibly safe to incredibly safe—far safer than walking down the street.

Notes and Disclaimers:

•This is my opinion, as an "industry insider" (Yes, a "self-proclaimed expert!")

•The Top 5 are in somewhat random order, rather than implied effectiveness. The exception is Number 1 which, in my opinion, has been the greatest improvement to aviation safety in the modern jet era.

5: TCAS, NextGen and ADS-B

Many improvements in aviation safety have come off the backs of airline tragedies. In fact, today's modern Air Traffic Control system traces its roots to the tragic 1956 midair collision over the Grand Canyon, when a United Airlines Douglas DC-7 struck a Trans World Airlines Lockheed L-1049 Super Constellation. All 128 on board both flights perished.

As a result, the Federal Aviation Act of 1958 created the Federal Aviation Agency (FAA, later renamed the Federal Aviation Administration,) which in turn greatly expanded the Air Route Traffic Control System, a series of ground-based radar controllers. Today, virtually every square inch of the contiguous 48 states enjoy radar control.

On-board, another wonderful advancement in technology has been TCAS. This on-board system warns of potential threats of other aircraft equipped with transponders (the electronic box that responds to ATC radar beacon interrogation), and will issue alerts. In addition, if two approaching planes have TCAS on board, the two boxes will coordinate with each other to come up with a vertical "solution," commanding one plane to climb and the other to descend.

A critical component of the US Next Generation Air Transportation System (NextGen) ATC system is ADS–B (Automatic Dependent Surveillance – Broadcast), which is already revolutionizing the WWII-era air traffic system by replacing ground radar with satellite-based GPS. This has vastly increased coverage area, bringing ATC and navigation to previously remote areas such as Northern Canada and Greenland, and giving both pilots and controllers "the big picture," in real time, of other traffic, weather, etc.

4: EGPWS—Enhanced Ground Proximity Warning System

Another wake up call for the industry came in 1995, with American Airlines Flight 965 into Cali, Colombia, which suffered a catastrophic "CFIT"—Controlled Flight Into Terrain. In nighttime, "severe clear" conditions, the experienced crew flew a perfectly good airliner straight into a mountainside, killing all 159 passengers and eight crew members.

The airplane was equipped with the revolutionary new "GPWS," Ground Proximity Warning System, which looks at radar altimeter data to predict a possible impact with terrain. However, the warning came too late, and the pilots were unable to out-climb the terrain.

Today's "Enhanced" GPWS gives the modern airliner a worldwide terrain database which greatly improves the safety margin, and even displays the potential hazardous terrain on the ND, or Nav Displays.

Along with TCAS, this has greatly aided the pilots' situational awareness.

3: LLWAS—Low Level Windshear Alert System

Another tragedy that led to great improvements in safety was the 1975 crash of Eastern Airlines Flight 66. Flight 66 was a victim of "windshear" caused by a thunderstorm microburst—that is, a rapid change in the direction and speed of the airmass in which it was flying, causing the Boeing 727 to stall shortly before landing, killing 113 of 124 on board.

A plane is simply a body moving through a fluid, much like a boat in a river. In any given configuration, there will be a minimum airspeed at which the plane can fly. The wind, like the river's current, can change. If the wind changes in speed and/or direction fast enough, the plane may theoretically lose that airspeed for a few critical moments before adjusting. In extreme cases, it may be too much from which an airplane can recover.

In the aftermath of Eastern, NASA developed a new system called LLWS-1 to detect these rapid changes in windspeed and direction, most often associated with microbursts. Over the years, this system has been improved and refined, including the incorporation of Doppler radar. If convective activity (i.e., thunderstorms) are detected in the area, LLWS advisories are given to arriving and departing aircraft.

Another recent addition to the cockpit has been predictive windshear detection systems, which use onboard Doppler weather radar to detect shears in precipitation ahead of the aircraft.

Number 2: RSWS—Runway Safety Warning System

The most deadly accident in aviation history remains 1977's Tenerife collision between two Boeing 747's, in which 583 people lost their lives. The accident was the result of a "runway transgression" when, in foggy weather, one 747 began the takeoff roll with another still on the runway.

Runway transgressions remain a hazard. To alleviate this threat, one of the most recent and delightful additions to the U.S. aviation safety system has been the Runway Safety Warning System.

RSWS uses transponder data from all aircraft to detect movement of an arriving or departing aircraft on a runway. When one is detected, red lights illuminate at runway intersections to alert transiting aircraft. Conversely, when an airplane is lined up at the end of the runway, ready to takeoff, and another is cleared to cross downfield, a row of red bars light up in front of the departing aircraft as a warning.

Currently, RSWS has been installed at several airports, and is rapidly expanding in use.

1: CRM—Crew Resource Management

In some ways, technology has advanced aviation safety to the point where the human pilots themselves have become the airplane's greatest liability. This has prompted some nincompoops to suggest the safest cockpit may be the one with no pilots.

I vehemently disagree with this absurd statement.

While humans may be the airplane's greatest liability, they also remain —head and shoulders above anything else—its greatest safety asset.

As we have tragically learned in the recent Germanwings 9525 crash, however, the human element can play a major role in aviation safety. Obviously, a homicidal pilot is exceedingly rare, but human factors still effect today's airline pilot. While the FAA and the public tend to treat us pilots as automatons that can fly without human issues, airline pilots are constantly facing such factors as fatigue, stress, and, yes, the need to "tend to one's physiological needs," as the FAA dryly puts it, by using the lavatory inflight.

In short, sad to say, we are still mortal humans.

"Welcome aboard our fully automated airplane!
Nothing can go wrong. Click! *Go wrong.* Click! *Go wrong . . . "*
Automation has drastically improved safety. But let's not take it too far just yet.

This being said—and I say again—the human pilot is by far the greatest "safety device" onboard your airplane. Drones and autopilots tend to grab the headlines ("Today's planes practically fly themselves, right?"), but the bottom line remains: as sophisticated as it is, today's modern airliner autopilot is nothing more than a fancy 3D cruise control. Can your car's cruise control drive you to the grocery store? Thought not.

And therein lies the most important safety issue in an airplane: Judgement—i.e., the thinking human mind.

Can a computer decide to ditch in the Hudson, or troubleshoot bad data for two hours in an A380 after the engine explodes and safely land the vastly overweight plane, saving over 400 passengers and crew, a la Captain Richard de Crespigny and his amazing crew aboard Qantas Flight QF32? (See, *Black Swan Event*, this volume.)

In case you're wondering, the answer is a definitive NO.

A computer can't even decide what to have for lunch.

Computers can *process*, but they can't *think*.

As a result, I believe, the "thinking" computer—the one that exercises (NOT "simulates") true judgement—is still a hundred years in our future.

The single-pilot airliner concept is nearly as absurd.

In my 35 years of flying, I have repeatedly observed that the two-pilot flight deck is the safest, most practical concept conceived. Two heads are exponentially better than one. Two pilots—a Captain and First Officer (NOT a "Pilot" and "Copilot," TUVM!)—can trap each other's errors, discuss fuzzy issues such as deviation around weather or diversion to take on more fuel, and assist each other when the lav juice hits the fan. (See, *Inflight Heart Attack*, this volume.)

I give a talk on CRM during the 2016 Airways Caribbean cruise.
Note the two important Captain-y types for my example!

I have talked extensively on my blog and in other articles about CRM, or Crew Resource Management, so I won't go into much detail here. Nevertheless, it remains a critical component to the vast improvement in aviation safety over the past few decades.

Captain Richard de Crespigny and I explore this topic in depth in his fascinating, three-part video interview (available in the ebook version of this volume, or at capnaux.com).

In short, however, CRM can be summed up in this: The old maritime tradition that "The Captain is God" has given way in recent decades to the concept that, "The Captain is in charge, leading a team of experienced, qualified professionals."

In other words, the Captain respectfully solicits the input from his valuable crew—especially his First Officer—before making critical decisions. In turn, a good captain creates a trusting environment wherein each crew member feels valued, and safe to speak up about any concerns.

For a fun analogy, look at the "evolution" of the captains in the *Star Trek* TV series. Originally, we had Captain Kirk, of the old "Captain is God" school. In *Star Trek The Next Generation*, however, we met Captain Jean Luc Picard, who not only valued his fellow crew, but actively sought their advice. Kirk may be the baddest-ass captain of all time . . . but Captain Picard was a *better* captain. For more on this subject, don't miss airline pilot and author Jean Denis Marcellin's excellent book, *The Pilot Factor*.

Honorable Mentions

Weather Radar—Around since WWII, weather radar has evolved into a highly sophisticated device which allows pilots to navigate around the stormy weather. Invaluable in today's cockpit.

Transponder/Mode C Transponder— Tracing its roots back to the original "IFF" (Identify Friend or Foe) system of WWII, the transponder is another wonderful tool that transmits aircraft data (identification, speed, altitude) to the interrogating signal, i.e., radar facilities. Mode C introduced the vertical portion of the equation, that is, altitude reporting.

EFIS—Electronic Flight Instrumentation Systems—The EFIS system consolidates the six standard flight instruments of yesteryear into one CRT or LED (i.e., "TV") screen, helping today's pilot to more easily fly on instruments. Moreover, the EFIS is incorporated into the autopilot, which in turns increases safety by relieving the pilot of the burden of mundane flying tasks and frees up his or her attention to take in "the Big Picture."

SECTION 3: Honoring our Military

Portrait of Petty Officer Richard Auxier, my father.
He served as a radar technician aboard the destroyer USS Preston in the
South Pacific during WWII.

LCDR Leland Shanle: Phantom Phlashback

Lieutenant Commander, USN (Ret); Airline Pilot; Author

Chilling with the Lt. Commander at Oshkosh 2015

"We continued to plummet, like two eagles with claws locked in a death spiral."

I first met Leland "Chip" Shanle through our *Blogging in Formation* team. Upon reading his recent novel, *Code Name Infamy*, I got thoroughly hooked on his historical war fiction. Chip is not only a stellar writer, he's actually *been there, done that*.

That is, fly fighters off the pitching deck of an aircraft carrier.

"Tower, Bloodhound 101, flight of four, ready for takeoff."

"Bloodhound 101, Point Mugu tower, cleared for takeoff, runway 11."

Gesturing to my flight of four aircraft, I tapped my helmet over the ear, then held up five fingers, signaling to switch to Button 5 for departure frequency. Easing onto the runway, I hugged the right side, and lined up on a seam in the concrete. This gave the rest of my flight room to position on the strip behind me. Simultaneously, on Channel Five, I checked in the flight.

"Shantini Flight?" I asked.

"—Two."

"—Three."

"—Four."

Came the rapid response, confirming all four Phantoms were on frequency. Glancing left down the line, I watched all three angry looking F-4s glide into place off my left wing. I could see all three pilots. Oxygen masks on with visors down, they had the look of modern gladiators. Holding up two fingers, I made a circular motion with my left hand to run up the flight to 80% power. The aircraft squatted and belched thick black smoke.

Scanning the gauges as my power reached 80%, I watched the afterburner nozzle position gauges pucker to half open, checked the flight controls by moving the control stick, and then looked left, waiting for my flight to do the same. I gave a last visual inspection to Dash Two. A thumbs-up was passed up the line. When it got to Dash Two, he inspected my F-4N quickly and passed a thumbs-up back to me.

Kissing them off, I jammed the throttles to full military-rated thrust.

The J-79-GE-8 turbojets came alive. The RPM stabilized at 101%, the exhaust temp jumped above 550° C, and the after burner nozzles closed to a 1/4 position. I paused only long enough for the gauges to stabilize, then pushed the huge throttles outboard and forward.

Boom! Boom!

Tapping the right brake, I countered the slight asymmetry as the burners lit unevenly. The travel for the oversized throttles in the burner region was as far as it could go for basic military thrust. As the burners staged, I could feel all four manifolds program in the full 17,000 thousand pounds of thrust per engine.

I scanned the nozzle position one more time to make sure they had opened all the way. The combined 34,000 pounds of thrust began to push the 45,000 pound F-4N down the runway. Twenty one burner injectors fed the J-79s 1500 pounds of fuel a minute. As 150 knots flashed by on the airspeed indicator, I maintained a take-off attitude.

The F-4N left the runway so smoothly, the only indication was the AOA approach indicator lights blinking on, signifying that weight was off the wheels. I grabbed the large handle to snap up the landing gear and began to trim nose down, holding the Phantom a mere 5 feet off the ground as it accelerated. Reaching behind the throttle quadrant, I found the tiny handle and retracted the flaps. The acceleration was now dramatic; as I closed on the end of the runway, the airspeed hit 300 knots (345 MPH). I yanked the nose up to 45 degrees of pitch and cranked on a 60 degree angle of bank left turn. The vertical climb indicator (VSI) pegged at plus 6000 feet per minute, the maximum indication on the gauge. The actual rate of climb was 13,000 feet per minute.

I began to ease the nose down incrementally to maintain 300 indicated. As the aircraft stabilized, I glanced down to see Dash Four come off the deck and begin his aggressive move to get inside my radius of turn.

"Departure, Blood Hound 101 airborne, flight of four," I transmitted on the UHF radio.

Each aircraft had rolled at five-second intervals; Icky in Dash Two was already joining on my left wing. He had held his nose down until 350 knots, using the advantage to run me down. Mink, the section leader and in Dash Three, was spaced perfectly between Icky and Scudder in Dash Four. I eased the burner to the mid position to allow my wingman a power advantage as I continued the turn.

After nearly 3/4s of a circle, I smoothly rolled wings level, and eased the throttles out of burner, simultaneously lowering the nose to 10 degrees to maintain 300 indicated.

QF-4N, assigned to VX-30
Pilot: Leland Shanle
Photo courtesy Leland Shanle

I looked back at my wingman; Icky had crossed to my right side and was in tight. Mink and Scudder were joined as a section on my left, with a space left for Icky to cross back and forth if required. We were in Finger-four formation.

The flight passed overhead the field at 13,000 feet, joined and heading Southwest out to sea, never having left the 5 mile confine of the airfield.

"Blood Hound 101, switch LA center, button six."

"Flight, go."

"LA, Blood Hound 101, flight of four, climbing one five thousand."

"Roger, Blood Hounds, continue to climb flight level three, zero, zero."

'Shantini?"

"2", "3", "4".

After visually checking my wingman, I loosened the formation to cruise by making a hitchhiking motion over my shoulders. Crossing Santa Catalina Island, we checked left for our next nav point, San Clemente

Island, and leveled at 30,000 feet. I left the power at 97%, and accelerated the flight toward air combat.

"Bloodhound 101, LA Center, switch to Beaver control, 354.5."

"Flight, go."

In the UHF radio, I manually dialed the frequency to 354.5.

"Beaver Control, Bloodhound 101, flight of four Phantoms, checking in for your control."

"Roger Bloodhound, squawk 1001, have your section leader squawk 1002. Say tactical call sign."

I reached down and twisted in the numbers to our IFF/beacon, which would allow the controller to separate us from other aircraft.

"Flight lead, Shantini, section, Mink."

I pumped Mink's section into combat spread by slapping the canopy palm out. Mink immediately snapped into a hard turn, repositioning one mile abeam. We would be able to cover each other's "Six." We had to; we were now in Indian Country. Icky and Scudder slid back to a loose, tac-wing position, so we could maneuver at will.

"Shantini Flight, music on."

All four Phantoms activated their onboard radar jammers. We had the latest and greatest from the jammer shop at Point Mugu.

"Beaver control, picture?"

"Beaver holds two groups of bogeys; first group, 2 cappers, two zero zero, for 120 nautical miles, 25,000 feet. Second group of 2 capping one eight zero degrees for 100, 20,000 feet."

"Commit group two."

"Roger, Shantini snap one eight zero for bogeys."

The flight was now committed to the fighter cap 100 miles to our south. We had leveled our climb at 40,000 feet. It was time to convert some of that altitude into speed. I pushed the flight over and called for burner over the radio. We had been cruising at .9 Mach, or 90% of the speed of sound. When we pushed over and went full burner, we punched through the speed of sound rapidly. I eased the throttles out of max burner to maintain our pre-briefed speed of 1.3 Mach.

"BRA?"

The transmission was a simple request for Bearing, Range and Altitude of the bogeys to whom we were committed.

"Two F-18 Hornets, bearing 1-8-5 degrees, range 80 miles, angels 20,000 feet."

We pressed in adjusting the heading to 185. The J-79s were consuming 1000 pounds a minute now.

"Declare!" I transmitted.

"Bandits, hostile, you are weapons-free."

"BRA."

We got the new distance, and knew radar guided missiles would be in the air.

"Shantini, Action!"

I broke hard to the right, knifing to 90° angle of bank and pulling 6 g's. Mink broke left, both of us descending to get the bogeys radar looking down. Once in our maneuver, we went full burner rolled wings level, and pulled 6 g's (six times the force of gravity) straight up.

We went from 15,000 feet to 30,000 in a matter of seconds, then pulled back toward the bandits. The maneuver, we knew, would trash the radar guided missiles and get us out of the bandits' radar scan.

"BRA?" I forced out over the strain of 6 g's.

"Zero-three-zero, at seven miles, 20,000."

I stuffed the nose and used the altitude to get my speed back.

"BRA?"

"Zero-one-zero, at five miles, 20,000." The controller's voice grew excited as we closed for the kill.

"Shit, I must be blind you got him?" I asked Ray, my backseater (Weapons Officer), over the intercom system (ICS).

"11 O'clock low, moving right to left!"

"Talley!" (In sight.)

"Shantini's Judy."

The transmission meant we had sight and didn't need the controller's calls anymore.

At max range, we got the rattlesnake tone of Sidewinder acquisition. I switched to our secondary radio which was tuned to shot-common frequency.

"Fox two," I transmitted. The radio code word for a heat-seeking missile launch.

"Clock is running," Ray called from the back seat.

We continued to close with a 200 knot advantage. In the heart of the envelope, we called another shot.

"Fox two."

F-4 Phantoms
Photo courtesy Ted Carlson

This time, the Hornet reacted. He broke hard to the right, chaff and flares exploding out of his belly in a desperate attempt to break missile lock. He obviously did not have us in sight, because he broke the wrong way and sweetened up the shot. Too bad, so sad.

"Time out, shot one," Ray deadpanned from the rear cockpit.

"Fox two, time out kill, F-18, 20,000 feet,

heading north."

"GUN-FIGHTER 112 YOU ARE KILL-REMOVED, EGRESS FIGHT WEST," the God-like voice transmitted over the shot-common frequency.

"Where is his damn wingman?" I asked.

"No Talley."

I scanned in phase with the Hornet we had just killed.

"Talley."

I gasped as I yanked on 8 g's.

The second F-18 was 10 degrees nose low in a high-g turn to the right. He was almost 90 degrees off our heading, showing pure planform.

"Shoot him, Shantini!' Ray grunted under the heavy g.

"I can't, he's out of the envelope. I'm closing for a gunshot."

We continued a descending turn, max burner at 8 g's. His planform remained under the piper of my gunsight. The world whirled in the background, but the gunsight picture remained unchanged.

"Why is this knucklehead arcing? Check our six for a wingman."

"Six clear, shoot him before he gets a clue."

It now only took 4 g's to hold the piper on his aircraft. At 3,000 feet, I eased the throttles out of burner and then to idle. I put the piper on the spot where the wings met the fuselage; I was pulling a lot of lead pursuit.

"Piper on, trigger down, tracking…….tracking….."

Went over shot common.

The Hornet driver finally saw us. He wrenched on a spiraling break turn, nose low. We were already at 15° angle of attack and pulled to 18° to keep the piper on. With the angle of attack past 15, I could no longer use the stick to turn the aircraft by using the aileron. If I tried, the F-4 would depart controlled flight, so I stomped the right rudder to roll with the Hornet. Our nose buried. I had to keep the piper on to achieve a kill because we were going to overshoot in close, big. If I didn't get the kill, he would reverse his turn and jump in my knickers. The Hornet was a far superior fighter; it could out-turn my old Phantom by a factor of two. I had sold the ranch to get the shot. If I gooned it, we were toast! At 1500 feet, I moved the piper to his helmet.

"Tracking….tracking…."

We continued to plummet, like two eagles with claws locked in a death spiral.

Five seconds elapsed with our piper on the flailing Hornet.

"Gun kill, F-18, right hand spiral, passing 15,000," we transmitted as we overshot the Hornet's fight path 500 feet aft.

"GUN FIGHTER 115 YOU ARE KILL-REMOVED, EGRESS FIGHT WEST," boomed over shot common.

"Shit that was close!"

Pointed straight down, I executed a half roll and pulled 4 g's toward a heading of south, smashed the throttles back to full burner and transmitted.

"Icky, take combat spread."

Our wingman had faithfully hung with us through the entire fight. He started to take position, one mile abeam, while we were still pointing straight down. By the time we pulled out at 5,000 feet, he was in combat spread and we were supersonic again.

"Beaver, snap vector to mother."

Mother was the aircraft carrier. It was the target of this mission and we intended to sink it.

"Mother bears one seven zero at 125 miles."

I checked the flight ten degrees to the left, steadied up 170, and continued to descend to 1,000 feet.

"BLUE BIRD, BLUE BIRD, BLUE BIRD." Came over shot common.

"Shit, the Aegis class cruiser is shooting at us! Hang on, Ray!"

"BLUEBIRD" transmitted over shot-common frequency meant the Aegis Class Cruiser had entered the fight. Not good!

The Aegis class was an SM-2-ER shooter, a particularly nasty Surface-to-Air Missile (SAM). The Spy-1 radar system could literally guide a boatload of missiles.

"Icky, let's high g barrel roll right."

"GO!"

Both Phantoms simultaneously pulled 4 g's straight up, then began a right roll while maintaining the pull. Passing through wings level on the horizon, we were inverted and I was in trail on my wingman. We continued to roll and pull through the nose-low portion of the maneuver, ending up on the same heading we had started. I had bet the 3-axis maneuver, coupled with the jammers, would break lock on the Spy-1. Now it was time to hide.

"Icky let's go for the deck."

We dropped to 100 feet above the waves. At 750 knots (860 MPH,) things happen fast. We boomed past an Oliver Hazard Perry class destroyer. *The floating single point of failure*, we called it. One screw (propeller), one power plant, one SAM launcher, one of everything. We knew it was no threat; it was a ship conceived and designed by penny-pinching bean counters, forced on the Navy by Congress. Basically useless. We didn't even bother to take evasive action.

"BRA to Mother?"

"165 for 50," came the response.

We checked left for 5 degrees and pressed the attack.

"Stand by for pop."

"Pop."

We heaved on 5 g's pulling up, then snap rolled inverted and put 5 back on. Once the nose was back on the horizon, we rolled upright. Mother, a USS Aircraft Carrier, was in our weapons envelope and in sight.

"VAMPIRE, VAMPIRE, VAMPIRE."

We transmitted over shot common; it meant we had put air to surface missiles into the air. Now, we would simulate the missiles by dropping back to the deck and closing on the ship. I flipped the radio to the Air Boss freq for the carrier.

"Boss, Bloodhound 101, two Phantoms for fly by, port side, bow to stern."

"Cleared Bloodhounds, keep it sub-sonic, heads up for the plane guard in the wake, you are clear to depart in the vertical."

I eased the throttles out of burner and climbed the flight to 500 feet. The Phantom was a Cadillac supersonic, but it was an unruly beast in the transonic region (.92-.96). Once we decelled to 600 indicated, around .9 Mach, we descended back to 200 feet. The Boss had cleared us for a fly-by from right to left, down the left side of the ship. He also gave us a heads-up for the helo behind it, and permission to depart straight up. Air Bosses were Naval Aviators who weren't flying anymore; they were ship's company but still liked a show.

We flashed past the ship, lighting the burners and pulling pure vertical. Unloaded (zero g), we climbed like a scalded dog. With no g on the Phantoms, the wings produced no lift and thus minimal drag, so we were literally a pair of rocket ships. I couldn't resist, and accentuated the zoom climb with a couple of aileron victory rolls. All good things must come to an end; we had battled gravity and achieved a temporary victory, but ultimately gravity would not succumb. At 350 indicated, I pulled the nose back to the horizon, rolled upright and headed north at 20,000 feet. The mission was not complete yet; we had to egress now. The Fighter cap we came through would not be happy at our success. We were going to have to fight our way out.

"Beaver, picture between Shantini and Texaco?"

Texaco was the KC-135 inflight refueler orbiting 200 miles north. Our personal gas station.

Photo courtesy Ted Carlson
Pilot: Leland Shanle

"Section bandits at angels three five zero, for 100, HOT!"

Hot meant they were pointed at us and closing.

"Shit Ray, it looks like we are going to have to fight our way out."

"Should be fun," was his emotionless response over the ICS.

"Icky, say state." I was asking how much fuel he had.

"6.8"

I looked down at my state; it was close.

"Shit, we don't have the gas to screw around, Ray."

"Icky, go stealth."

My options were: A, blow through the Hornets and run away, or B, turn with them and hope for an escape opportunity. I didn't really have the gas for either, and we definitely didn't have the gas for A. So, I chose stealth mode.

Stealth was an old Phantom trick. We went to idle on one engine, and minimum burner on the other. The Phantom had a nasty characteristic. It smoked like a bug truck. Long black lines of smoke would point to where you were if you had any power besides idle or burner selected. The first fighter to gain sight had a huge advantage. By going stealth, we got rid of the smoke, conserved fuel, and kept our airspeed close to cornering speed.

"BRA."

"3-4-0 at 55 angels 15."

"Check ten left."

I eased the nose down to get to 15,000 feet. We had to keep them in close to prevent giving them space to turn on us. Our speed built to 550 indicated in the descent. We were over 100 above our cornering speed, but could not come out of stealth mode this close.

"3-4-0 at 30, angels level."

They were two minutes out at our combined closing speed. Ray and I were heads-up, trying to get sight of the tiny Hornets.

"Talley!"

We were going to pass inside of a few hundred feet, at a combined 1,000 MPH. I decided to pull him into the phone booth to see what he had. I jammed both throttles to full burner and wrenched on 8 g's in an early turn.

Air combat is 80% mental. I wanted to see if this guy was a fighter pilot, or just some dude who flew around in fighters. I put my nose on him and pulled.

He was a fighter pilot. His F-18 matched my move with a 9 g pull, the air above his wings depressurized so violently it turned to cloud. We were going to pass very close, neither surrendering in our little game of chicken. At the merge, he rolled nose low and squatted in an incredible turn. We passed so close, we were both shaken by a huge jolt of turbulence created by our shock waves.

"Yee-Haaww!" came over my ICS.

It looked grim. He was kickin' my ass in the turn. Time to stop fighting his fight. I unloaded and snapped to wings level, then yanked the 8 g's right back on. The sun was high; I had to get into the sun before he shot me. As the nose reached pure vertical, I unloaded and held it directly in the sun. Cranking my head around, I watched the Hornet complete its eye-watering turn. He put his nose right on us, following us up hill. I was betting that he had come to the merge at his corner speed of around 310 KIAS. I knew that, with a turn on like I just witnessed, even using gravity, he was bleeding airspeed like a stuck pig. I held my nose in the safe zone of the sun, also bleeding airspeed like a stuck pig.

He couldn't shoot me; his heaters wouldn't lock on me in the sun, and we were outside of gun range and inside of radar-guided missile range. We hung nose up, waiting to see who fell first. My gamble payed off; the Hornet began to fall to the earth below. I took a quick snapshot of my airspeed: it was still 270, enough to get my nose down first. Burying the stick in my lap, I gave up everything I had left to pull the nose down.

The Hornet had hit zero airspeed and was now just a falling leaf. He was venting fuel which verified that. I got lucky; he was falling belly up, sweeping his tail pipes toward me. With the cool ocean in the background even if he went to idle, my heaters would track.

I got tone and sent two his way.

"Fox two, Fox two."

"Icky's Joker."

"Roger, bug out north."

Joker meant he had enough fuel to get to the tanker and re-fuel, but only if we left now. Otherwise, he would have to *bingo*—emergency divert to San Clemente Island. We headed North, burying the nose to let gravity give us airspeed as we ran for our lives. We were on the deck again, indicating 580 knots.

"Beaver," I called. "Bloodhounds are bugging out North. Check six."

The second Hornet was still alive. We were betting he, too, was low on fuel and couldn't give chase in burner.

"Six clear," was the welcome response that came over our headsets.

With our six clear, which meant no one was chasing us, there was no need to stay low. The higher we went, the better fuel economy we would get out of our J-79s. It was past time to find the tanker. We needed gas, and we needed it now.

I pulled the nose up to zoom climb the flight. We stayed at military-rated thrust, but didn't dare touch the afterburner. At our low fuel weight, I figured 325 would be a good climb speed. As our indicated bled down, I lowered the nose to hold a steady speed of 325. The zoom got us to 17,000 feet rapidly. After lowering the nose, we stabilized in a climb at approximately 6,000 feet per minute. The higher we climbed, the lower our fuel flow gauges indicated.

During the climb, I porpoised the nose by moving the stick fore and aft. Icky saw the tail movement; it was a silent signal to rejoin the flight in close formation. He closed in tight. I asked his fuel state with a hand signal. He held up four fingers first, then five. His answer meant 4,500 pounds of fuel. Leveling the flight at 25,000 feet, I figured we were fat on gas and headed for the tanker.

"Beaver, Bloodhounds, say tanker posit."

"Texaco bears 3-3-5 at 140 miles."

I set the fuel flow to 3,000 pounds per engine, 100 pounds a minute. Quick math told me we'd burn 2,000 enroute and we'd be on the tanker with 2,500 pounds. That left us 5 minutes to get fuel from the KC-135. Plenty of time.

"Hey Ray, I got us on the tanker with two point five. Check my math will you."

"I got the same Shantini."

"Cool, thanks."

We settled in for a leisurely cruise to the tanker, lost in our own thoughts on a glorious day. Off the left wing stretched the Pacific Ocean for as far as the eye could see.

Photo courtesy Leland Shanle
Pilot: Leland Shanle

Off our right wing was the coast of California in the distance, and San Clemente Island in the foreground. I felt a chill as my sweat-soaked flight suit cooled in the high altitude air. I turned up the temperature on the cockpit heat, and then went back to daydreaming.

"Bloodhounds, Texaco 3-3-0 at 15."

We were close; time to pull my head out. I scanned the horizon, but couldn't see the big tanker. He was at 22,000 feet, so I wasn't worried about hitting him. But I knew there were other aircraft in the area. I continued to scan. No tanker, but I picked up smoke trails; at the end of them were two Phantoms. OK, there was our other section, but where was the tanker? Then I noticed they were tanking. It drove home how the smoke trails gave away our position. They were literally within 30 feet of a converted Boeing 707, and I saw the F-4's first.

"Bloodhounds are visual, flight go Texaco frequency."

"Texaco, Bloodhound 101, flight of two Phantoms, noses cold, switches safe." That meant our radar was off and armament switches were set to safe. Our test models didn't have radar but the Tanker Bubbas wouldn't know that.

"Bloodhounds cleared to observation."

We found the tanker, one problem solved. However, we needed to get in the basket fast or we would be in deep *kimchee*. And, as always, there was a line at the gas station.

We were tight on fuel. We had five minutes to get some more, otherwise we would have to Bingo to San Clemente Island. A Bingo profile is an emergency; it has to be done exactly for you to make it to your divert without running out of gas. It is also an admission that you, as the flight lead or *wingie*, screwed up; you failed to manage your fuel. Naval Aviation has an old saying, "better to die than look bad." I knew Icky's fuel state was lower than mine.

"Hey Mink, we are a little tight over here," I transmitted.

"Roger that," was his transmitted response as he backed out of the re-fueling basket.

The Tanker Bubbas were listening in and knew the score from years of experience dealing with desperate fighters running out of fuel.

"Bloodhound Lead, you are cleared to pre-contact."

"Roger. Icky, cross under and take pre-contact. Get a quick 1,000 pounds."

He didn't need to be begged. He was already closing on the basket.

"Cleared contact," the Boom Operator transmitted.

Icky was in the basket and taking fuel within ten seconds. Our fuel continued to burn at 100 pounds a minute. I had three minutes left until an emergency divert. Ray's voice came over the ICS from the rear cockpit.

"Bingo from this altitude and distance is two-point-one."

I thought, "Great, we are moving away from our bingo air field." Now I had two minutes. Icky backed out and moved away. I didn't wait for the clearance from the Boomer. As Icky slid to the right, so did I, inch for inch at the same rate.

"Cleared contact."

Time to joust with the Iron Maiden.

Naval Aviators called the basket on a KC-135 the "Iron Maiden," because it was very user un-friendly. The Air Force and Navy had totally different concepts in aerial refueling. Air Force planes would line up behind the tanker, maintaining a normal formation, and then the Boom Operator would position a probe and extend it into a receptacle on the receiving aircraft. The Navy extended a basket that was shaped like a lamp shade with metal feathers that expanded when deployed. The feathers, or vanes, would keep the basket steady. Unless a Sea Service Pal banged the basket up trying to get into it, then it would move around. The basket was attached to a long hose that was reeled out from a tanker, or a tanker pod, called a buddy store.

The concept was simple; the pilot would position behind the tanker, fly his probe into the center of the basket, push forward to lock it into the coupling, then push the hose back into the tanker/buddy store until a light turned green then the tanker would transfer fuel. The key was to fly your position off the tanker, NOT the basket; because the basket would move, pushed by the bow wave of the receiving aircraft. You had to be precise and smooth. If you hit it too hard, a shock wave would go up the hose to the tanker, then back down, snapping off your re-fueling probe tip. Not good. If you hit off-center, the basket would bend then whip free, possibly coming through your side windscreen, also not good.

The KC-135 did not have a reeled basket; instead, they attached a large metal basket onto the Air Force boom. It was connected by turnbuckles at the boom attach point and the basket attach point. It was very unforgiving, thus the Iron Maiden nickname. The pilot had to perfectly balance the basket, and then hold a bend in the hard hose. Some pilots would rest the hose on the nose of their aircraft to hold it steady.

Each aircraft was different, and some were harder than others. The EA-6B, for example, was a great tanking aircraft. The probe was out in front of the pilot, easy to see and the aircraft was very stable at 250 knots, the normal tanking speed. The F-4 was not so great. The probe came out of the side of the aircraft, out of the view of the pilot. So, you either had to sneak a peek or fly the basket where you knew the probe was—the brail technique. The F-4, especially the QF-4, did not like to fly below 300 knots. In fact, it was one of the few aircraft that had a waiver from the FAA to fly above 250 knots (up to 300) below 10,000 feet when under IFR control. The Q had a very light nose because the radar had been pulled. To get the aircraft into (barely into) the minimum controllability window for CG (center of gravity), we had to carry fake concrete-filled missiles in the forward two fuselage missile stations. As the fuel tanks filled, the CG would move, and the already-squirrelly F-4 would get worse.

The author with his warbird, a Nanchang CJ-6A.
Photo courtesy David Shanle.

The bottom line was, as the Phantom filled, the AOA (angle of attack) would hover around 11.7 units. With an AOA at 12 units, the Phantom would pitch up uncontrollably. It was quite a sight (and ride) to see a QF-4 depart off the boom of a tanker. It always got the attention of the boomer!

It was with all this in mind and one minute to work with that I flew toward the basket. I should have been conservative, but I just couldn't resist a little bullshit bravado. I waited to flip the switch on the Phantom's refueling probe to time the extension, so that it fully extended and locked into place just as I plugged it into the basket.

"Good flow," the boomer transmitted.

I took a quick 1,000 pounds, then we all cycled back through the tanker until we were all topped off. We re-formed and turned south for another attack on the Fleet.

One day in the life of a Naval Aviator; we took it for granted that it would never end.

I only miss it when I breathe . . . .

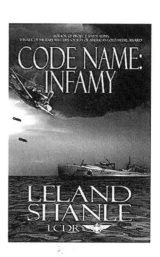

LCDR Leland C Shanle, Jr. retired from the US Navy in 1998. He is the author of the award winning Aviator *Series (*Project Seven Alpha, Vengeance at Midway and Guadalcanal, ENDGAME in the Pacific *and* CODE NAME: Infamy*).*

*He has been a major motion picture technical advisor (*Pearl Harbor, Behind Enemy Lines, xXx, Day After Tomorrow *and* Stealth*), and his company, Broken Wing, was behind Discovery Curiosity Series,* PLANE CRASH.

Currently, he flies the B-777 for American Airlines and a war bird (Nanchang CJ-6A) for fun.

Books available at lelandshanle.com

Major Rob Burgon: Airborne Assassins

Former F-22 and F-16 Fighter Pilot; Airline Pilot

"I focus on the bandit and not on the crushing power of my 9-g turn. The F-22's gun is my only remaining weapon."

Another one of our *Blogging in Formation* pilot-writers, Rob comes to us from the fighter jock world. I love his stuff, because he puts you right in that hot seat, pulling multiple g's and splashing hostile bogies. But don't listen to me rambling on about this; let's hear from the Top Gunner himself!

The gold-tinted canopy of my F-22 Raptor motored closed, isolating me from the noise of the Auxiliary Power Unit (APU) operating just a few feet aft of the cockpit. The displays are slowly waking up with power from the auxiliary generator—it will only be a few minutes before the powerful Pratt & Whitney F-119 Turbofan engines are roaring to life. I pause for a brief moment to reflect on how lucky I am to be sitting in control of the world's most lethal Air Dominance aircraft. My cerebral moment is interrupted by the voice of my crew chief crackling over the aircraft intercom.

"Alright, sir," says my crew chief, "we're all ready to go down here. I'll clear off when you're ready."

"You're cleared off chief," I reply. "Thanks for the start."

"No problem, sir. Good luck out there, and happy hunting!"

I smile as I check my formation in on our flight discrete frequency. With my three wingmen all on channel, I call for taxi clearance and work my flight into the line of aircraft flowing towards the two runways of Nellis Air Force Base, Nevada. Over 100 aircraft are participating in today's Large Force Exercise (LFE), and my four-ship is responsible for air-to-air escort of a strike package consisting of B-1 and B-52 bombers, F-15Es, and A-10s. It is a complex mission, and I know I need to be at the top of my game to make sure the mission is safely executed. Even though our aircraft are not loaded with live missiles, the threat of a midair collision lingers in the back of each pilot's mind.

We get airborne, climbing effortlessly into the cloudless, azure sky. En route to the fight airspace, we hop from one controlling agency to another, eventually ending up with our tactical controller, call sign Darkstar. There is no chatter on our flight discrete frequency; each flight member is focused on the mission ahead of us. There will be time for chitchat later as we regale each other with tales of airborne heroism after the mission in the squadron bar.

I check the clock as I turn my four-ship to the west, focusing our tactical sensors in the direction of our objective. Our vulnerability period—the time during which we will be responsible for mission accomplishment (also known as the vul)—is about to kick off.

Utilizing operational communications brevity terms, I ask the controllers onboard the E-3 AWACS to provide a verbal description of the location and number of airborne enemy fighters. The large dome radar on the AWACS turns slowly several miles behind us, painting an electronic picture of the battlespace.

"Raptor 1, Darkstar, picture: six-group wall. North group, bullseye two-eight-zero, fifty, fourteen thousand, hostile, heavy, four contacts…"

The Air Battle Manager proceeds to provide my escort package with a rundown of our airborne threats. Each pilot compares the radio communication to what he sees on his displays. Once Darkstar finishes providing the tactical picture, each pilot goes to work targeting and shooting his assigned group.

The initial volley of shots takes place beyond visual range. Some of the bandits execute a 180-degree turn, called a drag, as a defensive measure against the missiles coming their way. They have no way of knowing if the maneuver will work, and most won't survive the initial shots. I check the position of the strike package, which has started its push towards the target area. I check my flight's weapons and fuel states to find that we still have plenty of both.

In the few quiet seconds following our initial attack, I make a quick radio call to our tactical controllers and my flight, letting them know our status and our next plan of action.

"Darkstar, Raptor 1, weapons green, fuel green. Raptor 1 and 2 reference North CAP, Raptor 3 and 4 reference South CAP."

My four-ship splits up to provide 360-degree coverage of the target area, ensuring it is safe for the strikers to enter and drop their weapons. The geographic location where I will orbit with my wingman is called a Combat Air Patrol, or CAP. Once established in our CAP, high above the strikers, we prioritize our sensors to the enemy airfields nearby, only to see a massive launch of hostile aircraft intent on destroying our strikers. The radios erupt with chatter as the tactical controllers alert the pilots of the danger.

My wingman and I go to work in the South CAP, targeting and shooting the bandits as they seem to belt feed off the airfield.

It is only a matter of time before I'm out of AIM-120s, the only beyond-visual-range weapon I am carrying. With a closure rate in excess of 1,000 miles per hour, I am quickly approaching visual range with a two-ship of bandits. I push up on my Weapons Select Switch to put an AIM-9 missile in priority.

My only two missiles left—the heat-seeking, short-range AIM-9 missile —is used in the visual area, which requires me to execute a close-range intercept. In the F-22, performing a stern-conversion intercept to the six o'clock position of an unaware bandit is relatively easy. Undetected by the fire control radars of two F-16s simulating a Su-27 Flanker, I saddle up in a Weapon Engagement Zone (WEZ) and fire my last two missiles at the bandits.

"Raptor 1, Kill two-ship off the South Regen, bullseye two-three-zero, fifty-four, eight thousand." My radio call has notified our Range Training

Officer (RTO) that I have employed ordnance against two airborne contacts and have met the criteria for a kill. Without live weapons on the jet, I must utilize the embedded training software to simulate missile shots and let the RTO make the decision if the bandits die or if they will continue for training.

"Copy kill two-ship," replies the RTO. "Southern alive."

The RTO has let one of the bandits live. The live bandit is now a threat to our strike package. With only a few hundred rounds of 20MM bullets left, I push towards the enemy aircraft to attempt a gunshot. Suddenly, I see the bandit aggressively bank his aircraft into me; a maneuver called a break turn. I must time my execution of a similar maneuver just right to capture the bandit's turn circle and remain offensive. The dogfight is about to begin.

"Raptor 1, anchored, bullseye two-four-five, forty-nine, Remington," I say over the Blue Fight Frequency. The radio call is intended to let my flight mates know that I have merged with a bandit and have the F-22's gun as my only remaining weapon.

The crushing power of 9 g's (nine times the force of gravity) is all but imperceptible as my focus is on the bandit and not on the suffocating force pushing me into the ejection seat of my F-22. With both throttles parked in full afterburner and my jet sustaining over 400 knots in the downhill turn, I don't have time to be grateful for the ATAGS (g-suit) helping to keep me conscious. I barely notice the stinging in my arms—a result of the capillaries in the skin bursting from the blood pushed to them by the force of the turn. No, my attention is across the turn circle on the bandit who has picked up a lucky tally on me and continues breaking defensively.

I wonder if he knows just how lucky he is. He would have been dead long before our merge if I had any missiles left. We are now more than one-half hour into our mission, with the strike package off target and beginning to head home. Being anchored in a dogfight against an enemy carrying several high off-boresight missiles is not the optimal situation for this Friday morning—or any morning for that matter. With the offset turn circles we are flying, it will only be a matter of time before I fly through the bandit's missile WEZ. Where is my wingman?

"Raptor 1, Raptor 2 is in from the north, five miles, supporting!"

The radio call from my wingman is music to my ears. I know he still has missiles on his jet and will be able to affect the outcome of this fight easier than I can on my own.

"Raptor 1 copies. Raptor 1 is engaged, offensive, low man in the stack," I reply on our flight discrete frequency.

"Raptor 1, PRESS!" With this single radio call, my wingman indicates he has both the bandit and me in sight, and that he knows who is who.

"Raptor 2, are you able to shoot?" This fight, although brief, is starting to put me dangerously close to bingo fuel. If I continue to drive into gun range, I will be snapping directly to home plate after my gun track and flying a minimum fuel profile to base.

"Raptor 1, affirm, come off right. Raptor 2's engaged your left seven o'clock slightly high, one mile."

I ease off my left-hand turn and find my wingman right where he said he was. The bandit has not seen him enter the fight. I key the mic and tell my wingman, "Raptor 2, PRESS!"

Within seconds, Raptor 2 fires an AIM-9M, and the fight is over. It ended just the way it was supposed to end, and much more quickly than if I had pushed into a gun WEZ.

With the strike package now safe, and the air-to-air escort package egressing the fight, I can't help but smile. The battle was hard fought, our skills were put to the test, and I'd like to think we proved our mettle.

War is not something that should be hoped for, but something for which we must prepare if it is thrust upon us. The Raptor has yet to fire an air-to-air missile in anger, and hopefully, that day never comes. Things will have gone terribly wrong in the world if the Raptor is drawn into a shooting match. The tenuous peace we enjoy in the world today can change in an instant, and if it does, the men and women who fly the F-22 will be ready to supply Air Dominance at a moment's notice.

Editor's note: I'm excited to inform you that Rob is about to publish his first book, a "tell-all" of the life of a Raptor pilot! Check this out:

Piano Burning & Other Fighter Pilot Traditions

The world of the fighter pilot is steeped in tradition. Over a century's worth of ritual, superstition, and lore permeates the life of modern combat aviators. Every time-honored tradition upheld in today's fighter squadron is infused with deep meaning and strengthens the bonds between our airborne warriors.

In Piano Burning and Other Fighter Pilot Traditions, you will be given a behind-the-scenes view of the combat aviator's world through the eyes of a modern-day fighter pilot. Get ready to explore the sacred origins of these customs and rituals as practiced by the men and women who fly the deadliest fighter aircraft in the world:

•Friday in the Fast Jet Business
•Roll Call

- The Legend of Jeremiah Weed
- Fighter Pilot Songs
- Squadron Bar Games
- Tactical Call Signs
- Mustaches
- Challenge Coins
- Apologies
- Piano Burnings
- Debriefs

This book is written for an audience of all ages. Whether you are a kid contemplating a career in the fast jet business or a retired fighter jock looking to share memories of your world with your family, Piano Burning has got you covered.

Check six!

Major Rob Burgon is a combat-experienced fighter pilot with over 2,000 hours of multi-engine turbine time logged in the F-22, F-16, and T-38. The bulk of his military flight time has been logged as an Instructor Pilot.

Rob has recently accepted a pilot position with a major airline and is currently transitioning to civilian life after 12 years of Active Duty military service. He continues to fly fighters with the United States Air Force Reserve on a part-time basis.

Rob is an accomplished writer, freelance author, and member of the "Blogging in Formation" team. He has produced numerous training documents for the United States Air Force, and in his spare time runs his own blog, TallyOne.com and co-hosts Slipstream Radio. He is currently working on two of his own aviation-related non-fiction works.

Rob lives with his wife and three children in Florida, where he has lived since his recent separation from Active Duty.

Photos in this piece courtesy of the author.

Captain Alan Carter: Evacuating Tripoli

Global Heavy metal driver; Humorist

"A Boeing 747 makes a huge and very inviting target."

Early in 2016, I had the great joy of sharing the Airways Cruise stage with Captain Alan Carter. We hadn't met previously, but had enjoyed each other's blogs from afar. I must say, Alan in person is even more zany, quick-witted and fun than even his words convey, as you may have seen from our Airways Caribbean cruise videos!

February 26th 2011, found myself sitting in my bijoux Baghdad residence which, once upon a time, served as a shipping container.

My accommodation was protected, not by smart, overdressed doormen, but instead by even smarter and politer ex-Gurkha guards wielding AK47s. My once-stylish hotel rooms were swapped for air conditioned containers with hot and hot running water; but I loved it. I could often be heard to say "It is what it is," and always with a smile on my face.

A little bit of background. I was employed by an Iraqi government department to head up a team flying their newly-purchased Boeing 747-400. Well, I thought it would be an adventure. And boy, it certainly was.

Suddenly, Skype sprung into life with a call from our beloved leader, Joe, in the United Kingdom.

"Alan, we have been told that 'YOU' have a flight to operate tomorrow," Joe exclaimed.

No big deal, that's what we were here for. However, from Joe's tone, I could tell he was building up to something.

"Alan, Prime Minister Maliki wants you to fly to Tripoli, Libya, and collect as many Iraqi Embassy staff, families and citizens as you can. Alan, you still there?"

Well, my hesitation was because Libya was in the midst of a violent civil war and Colonel Gaddafi was being hunted—and, unbeknownst to him, had only eight months left before being turned into a human sieve.

Home sweet shipping container home, conveniently located in the (rarely-bombed) centre of Baghdad's runways.

'*Cool*' I thought; a change of region for my family to follow on CNN news when trying to keep up to date with my latest movements.

My enthusiasm, though, was not often repeated by my family, who were deeply unenthusiastic at this prospect. They had become used to the fact that I was no longer based in a cosmopolitan western city, or by the banks of one of Italy's many beautiful lakes; but instead in the semi-secure area between Baghdad airport's two north-south runways.

Joe trying to explain that operating into the Libyan war zone on an Iraqi government-backed humanitarian rescue flight would be perfectly safe was, to be honest, met by me with more than a little disbelief.

Not surprising, really, especially after all of his previous assurances about our safety in Baghdad had fallen on deaf ears after two mortar shells landed nearby my compound whilst I was chatting on Skype with my daughter. She being in leafy Surrey and myself in sandy Baghdad, it was not a scenario that she wanted to become used to.

I was told that this threat of mortars was the reason why there was a gap between the walls and the bed, so that if the pictures fell off the wall, they wouldn't land on my head.

Why didn't they just move the pictures? Or was that simply another 'urban legend' amongst so many associated with this region?

US Choppers enroute to take care of a little "nuisance"— mortar fire onto the airport during my preflight.

Now, I had been to Tripoli before, using the airport as a place to fill up on cheap fuel whilst flying a Zimbabwe-registered DC-10 for an ex British Army Officer between my base southeast of Paris to destinations in Africa. So, I was familiar with the airport—but that was before the civil war.

The operation, however, almost stumbled at the first hurdle, as the Iraqi flight planning department led me to believe that they'd not heard of European Flow Control or their CFMU (Central Flow Maintenance Unit). Not really their fault, as it had been many years since they had operated outside of the Middle East region.

So, after a call to a friend of mine at the CFMU headquarters in Belgium, I (as diplomatically as possible) suggested that they re-file our flight plan, not through closed Libyan airspace as they proposed, but by the only approved entry point that the current political situation allowed. This meant that over-flight permits were required for Jordan, Egypt, Greece and Malta, as well as landing permission for Tripoli itself.

So, Joe—a highly experienced UK training captain and airline manager whom acted primarily as a consultant for this operation—spent the next 24 hours tirelessly to obtain these on behalf of the Iraqi Government, and Iraqi Airways, under whose AOC we were operating.

After an inevitable day's delay, he had obtained all of the necessary clearances as well as the specialised 'war zone' insurance required for this type of operation.

So, having suffered this delay to our flight whilst waiting for the necessary paperwork to be obtained, and receiving twenty thousand US Dollars in cash (which I had a hunch would not be sufficient to cover expected and unforeseen expenses), we were finally ready to depart.

The aircraft was catered for what we hoped would be a full load, and fueled to enable us to fly to Tripoli and back to Baghdad with extra reserves to cover any unexpected 'surprises'. Well, fuel here in Baghdad was virtually free, as it was literally coming out of the ground, and how much we carried was never questioned.

As often happened, but this time whilst conducting my external walk round inspection, a couple of mortars landed on the far side of the airport, targeting, as usual, 'French Village,' not far from the infamous Abu Ghraib prison.

There was almost always the sound of automatic gunfire as background 'music', whether coming from the firing ranges. Or "other sources." Initially alarming, but you soon became used to it, as you would bird song or traffic noise. In fact, one night it sounded like the 4th of July celebrations, as the Gatling guns tried to shoot down the incoming 'fireworks'!

So, hiding under the wing, I watched a couple of US helicopters set off to 'investigate' their source. In hindsight, not a perfect spot, as I had 150 tonnes of jet fuel above my head.

Sitting with me on the flight deck was my fabulous colleague, Marty, an American Captain who had a terrifically dry sense of humour. Behind us sat a full complement of cabin crew, sufficient security personnel who were all ex-special forces from the Iraqi army to protect us, as well as two ground engineers. We departed Baghdad on runway 33R for our 'adventure' to Tripoli.

Our routing took us west from Baghdad towards the Jordanian border, passing to the north of Petra and the Dead Sea and into Egyptian airspace, being careful not to cut the corner and stray into Israeli airspace for obvious reasons.

A beautiful day to go flying took us over the southern entrance to the Suez Canal where, looking down, I was amazed at how few ships were waiting to transit; maybe a sign of either the global economy or the uncertainty of this region's stability.

Heading further north, we flew over the densely-packed city of Cairo, which was too smoggy, unfortunately, to see the pyramids—in fact, I had never seen them from the air. We then coasted out over the city of Alexandria and into the eastern Mediterranean Sea.

A good time to eat my lamb kebabs and warm chips served by a member of our fabulous cabin crew, as we had about half an hour of peace and quiet before entering the busy European airspace, home to numerous charter flights dropping in and out of the beautifully scenic Greek islands; a type of flying which I had thoroughly enjoyed in many previous companies, almost too many to mention, but for whom I consider myself lucky to have worked.

I need to add here that, in all my years of flying, I have never met such a professional, friendly and conscientious group of cabin crew, who accepted whatever they were tasked with, always with a smile on their faces. I doubt if I shall have the good fortune to fly with a comparable group of friends and colleagues again, especially as I am predominantly flying the Boeing 747 freighter now.

No cabin crew on a freighter, just a load master and a ground engineer; not a skirt or sweetly perfumed young lady in sight, and not quite the same. Though, strangely, sometimes better.

With lunch over and the Greek border southeast of the island of Crete approaching, it was time to see if our flight would be accepted by European Air Traffic Control agencies. Yes, we had the required over-flight permits, but even so, we were still an Iraqi-registered aircraft flying under an Iraqi Airways call-sign, the first time in many years that such a flight had passed through this region.

I need not have worried, as we were cleared to enter and given a direct routing to a position south of Malta. I tempted fate by thinking that it was all running like clockwork.

I should have known better.

With our Flight Management Computers correctly programmed for the arrival onto Tripoli's westerly runway, utilising the Instrument Landing System there (that might or might not be working), Marty and I conducted a thorough arrival briefing, and escape plan should the need arise. Well, we were not overly sure what to expect; we had both seen the news as reported on various television channels.

The situation on the ground looked pretty ugly, and wasn't about to improve anytime soon.

We had already discussed the benefits of landing in either daylight or at night, and decided that both had their advantages and downsides, too. You see, we were used to operating into airports where there could be threats from the ground and understood what needed to be done.

So, a daylight landing it was to be, but a continuous descent approach would be flown, staying above 3,000 feet for as long as possible. This was the height that we considered to be safe from SAFI, or Small Arms Fire. Manpads, though, were an entirely different worry: those shoulder-launched missiles were as freely available in this part of the world as a Macdonald's Big Mac is in New York.

So, with all our arrival procedures complete and clearance to enter Libyan airspace obtained, we started our descent, and finished our last cup of coffee. We were handed over by the Maltese controller to a surprisingly chirpy Libyan one, who passed over the weather for Tripoli, gave us our arrival clearance, and asked us to pass on any information as to whether the ground-based navigation aids were actually working. He couldn't be sure if they were, or how long they would remain functioning. Yes, we were in Africa, where this was a 'routine' experience, but he nevertheless reminded us that we were also entering a hostile area.

Bombs on the Baghdad strip. All in a day's work.

Again, we need not have worried, as the ILS was functioning correctly, and so were the approach and tower control frequencies for Tripoli—for the time being.

Keeping our eyes peeled for anything out of the ordinary, unknown military aircraft, lasers or unfriendly items sent our way from the ground, Marty and I configured the aircraft for landing.

Going back to lasers, aircraft are, these days, being targeted too often by them, primarily by idiots on the ground who think that it is funny to try and shine them into the cockpit of aircraft, be this in the UK, the Canary Islands or many other countries. A foolhardy and dangerous thing to do, as it could blind the pilots—as happened recently to a Virgin Atlantic pilot on departure from London Heathrow—and lead to a less than satisfactory outcome to all on-board that particular aircraft. When it happened to me on the approach into an Iraqi airport at night, it tended to concentrate the mind and reminded me of the old saying, "It is better to be on the ground wishing you were in the air, than in the air wishing you were on the ground."

However, apart from a gusty wind and its associated turbulence, the approach and landing was uneventful, and we exited the runway and headed to our designated parking spot. I didn't realise how busy it would be here, with a multitude of aircraft arriving and departing on rescue flights.

I also didn't realise that, now, the fun was about to begin in earnest—especially as we were greeted by a pickup truck driven by a character waving a pro-Gaddafi green flag and shouting out associated Arabic messages, extolling the virtues of that regime, and down with the USA, down with England, etc. We decided it might be prudent that, for a while some of us became 'honorary' Australian citizens. Which we did!

I can't help but wonder what happened to this guy. But, that would be irrelevant, as we now had more important things to worry about, and a deadline that could not be extended. This deadline was dictated by our insurance company that would only give us cover for a maximum of three hours on the ground in a war zone, so we needed to get organised, find our 'passengers' and leave as swiftly as possible.

This would prove to be easier said than done.

Often, the flying part is the easiest of the tasks set for a pilot. It is the organisation and operation on the ground which requires the greatest skills, both in diplomacy and management, and this day would test both of these.

Annoyingly, my mobile phone would not work here on the ground in Tripoli, and my only means of communication with my boss in the UK and Iraqi Airways in Baghdad was through Stockholm Radio, using the HF network. Not ideal, so an alternative needed to be sourced to solve this problem, along with other problems which were starting to unfold on a minute-by-minute basis.

With various people boarding our aircraft and being searched by our Iraqi Airways security team, it soon materialised that, before anything could be done, we had to pay. This would be for navigation fees, landing charges, handling and parking charges, too.

So with a member of the Iraqi Embassy and a local Libyan 'handling agent,' I was whisked off to relieve myself of several thousand US Dollars.

I was accompanied on this task by a fabulous gentleman, again a member of our security team, who did a great impression of Lord Nelson, as he always kept his hand inside his buttoned up jacket. These guys carried weapons with two different types of magazines. One set had a blue tape around them, indicating these held ammunition which was 'safer' to use onboard an aircraft. The other sets would stop a charging elephant.

We were driven off to the flight planning and handling office. Now, I have been to many of these flight ops 'departments' in my career, but the sight of this one was something for which I was totally unprepared. It resembled a rundown squat used as a New York crack den and inhabited by some very untidy individuals. However, the Libyan staff here could not have been more helpful. They had nothing, their country was in meltdown, yet what they did have they wanted to share with me; a cup of 'chai' with them was an almost humbling experience.

One member of the local Iraqi Embassy staff kindly leant me his personal mobile phone, which was most welcome, and I was allowed to keep it for the 'duration.' I am sure he meant just a couple of hours, but I returned it two days later and with its credit exhausted.

Returning to my aircraft, it materialised that we only had 70 passengers, the problem being that there were so many checkpoints between the city and the airport, that it was becoming very difficult for the 'refugees' to make their way. This was compounded by the security
teams manning these checkpoints 'confiscating' their money, passports and

anything else which they took a fancy to, along with systematically beating them. We were then advised that it would be many hours before any more of our passengers would be in a position to board our aircraft.

We were advised that these 70 passengers would be removed from the airport if they did not board immediately. Now, I didn't want to board them just yet, as we were advised by the Iraqi Government that it would be unacceptable to fly to Tripoli and then only return to Baghdad with 70 passengers; it would have been a political public relations disaster.

However, I didn't want to lose those that we had, as there were many families with children. So, a group decision was made to board them and wait as long as we could.

After three hours on the ground and no hope of extensions to our insurance, time was running out. We had to leave, and with the option of returning to Baghdad being an unfavourable one, and a guarantee from the Iraqi Embassy staff that our remaining passengers plus the 70 we already had would be ready to depart the following day, I decided to offload those already on-board and depart for Tunis, which was only an hour away. There, we could come up with our next plan, and buy us some more time.

As a note, if we had taken these passengers with us, then we would have been impounded in Tunis, and no hope of returning to pick up all those we had left behind. It was an extremely difficult decision to make—one of the toughest in my thirty years as a pilot.

The decision was made to fly to Tunis, because we were very fortunate that our senior cabin crew member was himself from Tunis, and he had friends at the airport there. It was through him and Joe that we were able to organise our overflight permissions of Tunisia and our landing permit into Tunis. Again, it's who you know in this business.

So, with the surprisingly very understanding passengers disembarked and the aircraft pre-flight checks all completed, we started our engines for a departure to Tunis's Carthage International Airport.

Although the westerly runway was favoured by the surface wind, the entry onto this runway had been destroyed by mortars, so a back-track followed by a 180 degree turn at the poorly-lit runway's end would be required to take off in a westerly direction. It was now dark, and not wishing to take any undue risks, Marty and I decided that it would be prudent to accept a ten knot tailwind and depart using the full length available on the easterly runway. It was starting to turn nasty again, and a white Boeing 747 makes a huge and very inviting target.

After a thankfully uneventful take-off, we were cleared by Libyan air traffic control to fly direct to our exit point on the Libyan-Tunisian border. However, this would mean flying over the town of Zawarah, a coastal town west of Tripoli, which we had earlier been advised by Iraqi embassy personnel was experiencing hostile actions.

So, we instead decided on a northerly track between the eastern edge of Tripoli and the quaintly-named town of Castelverde, thus keeping us clear of Zawarah and its missile threats.

Climbing to our cruise altitude of 38,000 feet only took fifteen minutes, and, being handed over to Tunisian air traffic control west of the island of Djerba, we were cleared direct to a waypoint named Zahra, which was the initial approach fix for the arrival routing into Carthage airport when using the ten-thousand foot long runway 01.

A normal landing using just idle reverse and no auto-brakes ensued.

We customarily tried to use as little reverse thrust as necessary to minimise engine wear and foreign objects damage, accompanied with minimal braking to reduce brake and tyre wear, too. Our preference was to use the available runway length whenever possible and so reduce our maintenance costs as much as possible; with only one Boeing 747-400 in our company, we had little flexibility for unscheduled maintenance.

We planned to stay on the ground in Tunis for around sixteen hours, taking rest in the hotel and coming up with an alternative plan of action. During this ground time, the necessary landing and over-flight permits were obtained, Tunisian handling bills paid by a member of the Iraqi embassy in Tunis, and the aircraft was re-catered—most important!

The subsequent flight to Tripoli was uneventful. There were 210 passengers waiting for us on arrival, and after spending the last of my dollars, and donating all the catering which we could spare to the extremely grateful ground staff, we closed our doors and set off for home; well, Baghdad anyway.

A great adventure and very rewarding that we had removed so many families from harm's way; however, it's a question of "the devil you know." Tripoli or Baghdad—as we say, a "Hobson's choice," I suppose. Although, a year on, it seemed that Tripoli was actually a safer proposition than Baghdad. Though, now in 2016, where is safe? I don't know.

I'm no longer involved with the Boeing 747-400 operation in Baghdad. Since then, I have secured fantastic contracts flying the Boeing 747-400 for both an Azerbaijan and currently a Turkish company, subcontracted to airlines in Saudi Arabia and Qatar.

Yet another fabulous adventure, where I've been flying freight to destinations as diverse as Hong Kong, Kazakhstan, Afghanistan, the odd African country, as well as China and Europe.

I consider myself to be very lucky.

Captain Alan Carter has been an airline pilot for over 30 years, and has spent the equivalent of more than 2 years on the flight deck. He has flown the HS748, Boeing 727, Boeing 737, Boeing 747 and DC10 all over the world, from Baghdad to Seoul.

Captain Carter is a Columnist for Airways Magazine, as well as a contributing writer for Flight Global Working Week, and Airliner World.

He is also proud to say that he has the same number of takeoffs as landings in his logbook!

Alan can be reached at cla747@icloud.com.

All photos in this piece courtesy of the author.

SECTION 4: The Cap'n Strikes Back

Responsible Journalism and the Air Crash Du Jour
Originally published in Airways News

1: Op-Ed: Responsible Journalism and the Air Crash Du Jour

For our number one story of 2015, Captain Eric Auxier's Op-Ed stole the show. The 20 year A320 veteran pilot discuses how the media does not always report the "news" in lots of aviation stories, which was especially prevalent during the coverage of Germanwings 9525. Captain Auxier breaks down media coverage of aviation accidents and explains why it is not a good idea to speculate or report unconfirmed facts.

This sucker made the #1 Top News story of 2015 for AirwaysMag.com!

"Somewhere between Walter Williams and Brian Williams, we've lost that sacred mantra of journalism: that the public journal is a public trust."

For awhile now, I've been a regular Columnist for that amazing aviation magazine, *Airways* and its online counterpart, AirwaysMag.com. What's even more fun is I get to write Op Ed's for said online site, the more scathing the better. Well, I can scathe pretty well, especially when faced with incompetence or downright ignorance in the field of aviation.

After the Germanwings 9525 tragedy, the clueless media was at it again, irresponsibly "solving" the case before crash investigators had even extracted the Black Boxes. Worse, CNN's self-proclaimed "Aviation Expert" Richard Quest rudely shouted down two airline captains when they were hesitant to discuss security on worldwide feed. Sadly, the irresponsibility continued with the more recent EgyptAir 804, still missing at press time. In this latest episode, Quest had the audacity to discuss the best place to place a bomb onboard an aircraft. He defended himself on Twitter by stating that the terrorists already knew this stuff. True, perhaps, but what about the hundreds of amateur copycat wannabes?

Thanks again, Quest, for blatantly endangering lives.

This was not only my top blog post of 2015 on capnaux.com, but at nearly 8,000 Facebook shares, it was the top post of 2015 for AirwaysNews as well.

As a 20-year veteran of the A320 cockpit for a major U.S. airline, including the last 15 in the Captain's seat, I have cringed at the utter misrepresentation of aviation facts often disseminated by news outlets and their self-proclaimed "aviation experts" endlessly paraded across the TV screen after the latest air disaster.

Coverage of the tragic crash of Germanwings 9525 was no exception.

While today's news suggests that the First Officer deliberately flew his A320 into the ground, until the CVR (cockpit voice recorder) was found and analyzed, worldwide news sources had faced a dearth of data to report on a major news story, and instead filled the gaps with both fantastic, and fantastically inaccurate, fluff.

By nature, as we all wait breathlessly for any morsel of breaking news regarding the fatal crash, our subconscious can't help but race ahead, and fill the gaps between facts with speculation. In this hyperconnected age, this same speculative fill-in-the-blank occurs collectively, worldwide, via live, 24-hour news feeds such as CNN.

Worse, these very same reporters, who have zero experience with aviation, tend to let their own imaginations fly (excuse the pun).

In our "Quest" for accurate aviation reporting, why must we endure self-professed "experts" in lieu of real ones?

Modern disasters saw such storied gems as CNN anchor Don Lemon's "black hole theory" about MH370, promptly one-upped in absurdity by former DOT Inspector General Mary

Schiavo's reply that a "tiny black hole would swallow the entire universe." (See our AirwaysMag.com Op Ed, *"Mary Schiavo and the Clueless Press"* for more of her shenanigans.)

Graphs depicting the plane du jour are a comic cavalcade of inaccuracies, such as a four-engine A320, or a double-decker Boeing 737. And let's not forget such enlightening tidbits as, "Boeing 777 will struggle to maintain altitude once the fuel tanks are empty."

At least, so far, no news source has come up with a Germanwings equivalent of Captain Sum Ting Wong and First Officer Wi Tu Lo.

Seriously, however—and with the deepest condolences and respects to the victims and families of the Germanwings 9525 tragedy—these endless speculations and haphazard reporting have become blackly comical at best, and wildly irresponsible at worst. Families and loved ones of those lost tend to hang on every word disseminated by the international media, and somewhere between Walter Williams and Brian Williams, we seem to have lost that sacred mantra of journalism: that the public journal is a public trust.

To be sure, some highly qualified individuals occasionally grace the TV screen with their pearls of wisdom, such as international A330 pilot Karlene Petitt, author of *Flight to Success*. But for every expert, there seems to be some Ya-hoo whose sole qualification is that he watched Airport '77.

Covering all angles of a news story is one thing, but unhealthy obsession with a single aspect is another. For example, in the first 48 hours after the 9525 crash, news outlets were quick to question the design of the Airbus itself. Known for its high level of automation, this very same design philosophy has come under intense scrutiny. While somewhat justified in the aftermath of Air France 447 (see, *Understanding AirAsia 8501*, this volume), it is nevertheless human nature to fear the unknown and, like Stanley Kubrick's HAL 9000 computer in *2001: A Space Odyssey*, suspicion often falls first on that which is least understood.

When contacted for this piece, Karlene Petitt agreed: "Having flown the A330 around the world for six years, I will stand by the plane and fly it any time. The A330 is extremely stable, and the technology brilliant. It's only those who don't understand the technology, that have problems. It's not the plane. I suppose we fear what we don't know, but the Airbus should not be one of those fears."

Yes, mechanical things fail. Yes, an airplane with over 1 million parts and dozens of computers will need regular maintenance. During my recent Skype interview with Qantas A380 Captain Richard de Crespigny, author of QF32 and the captain aboard Flight 32 during an inflight engine explosion, Captain de Crespigny said, "If you want to fly a high-tech airplane, there is a responsibility to understand the systems. Because when those systems fail —and they do fail—it's up to the pilot to recover."

Indeed, the Airbus is one of the most high-tech airliners ever built. While it was specifically designed to allow a less-experienced pilot to safely operate, it is incumbent upon every pilot to understand these systems in order to overcome any possible event. But, really, this philosophy applies to any pilot and their aircraft. Regardless of aircraft type, safety always boils down to basic stick and rudder.

OK let's set the record straight on this whole Airbus thing. While the latest evidence for Germanwings 9525 points toward pilot suicide, even if this accident did prove to be a design flaw of the Airbus itself, the safety record still ranks the A320 family (A318-A321) in the top five safest airline models of all time. Odds of dying in an A320: 1 in 792 million flights.

Lifetime odds of dying in any airplane: 1 in 11 million.

Lifetime odds of dying in a car: 1 in 77.

The venerable news channel, in their—eh, "Quest" for accurate aviation reporting, enlightens the public yet again with another tidbit of wisdom.

Ironically, during an exhaustive CNN panel discussion by aviation experts, *Cockpit Confidential* author Patrick Smith offered that news channels should avoid obsessive over-speculation about plane crashes. In doing so, Smith says, it exacerbates the misperception of an increasing danger in the skies. Retired American Airlines pilot Jim Tilmon agreed, going further to voice his concerns about discussing—at length and on worldwide feed—security measures in place aboard the world's airlines.

Captain Tilmon was promptly shouted down by CNN's "resident aviation expert" Richard Quest. While Quest may have won the Association for International Broadcasting's 2014 "personality of the year," I fail to see how this qualifies him as an aviation expert. Best I can tell, his expertise in aviation stems from his possession of a very loud and obnoxious voice, and possession of a passenger seat on the last Concorde's flight.

I wholeheartedly agree with Smith and Tilmon's points, especially their concern over airline security. By their very nature, these issues are best left unearthed. By discussing these issues publicly, was airline security compromised? Perhaps not, but it seems we are treading a very hazardous line for the sole purpose of filling a few measly minutes of air time.

In this very column, in an Op Ed on MH370, airline captain Mark Berry, author of *13,760 Feet—My Personal Hole in the Sky*, said that speculation can be a good thing. I agree. But when speculation turns to conjecture, when fill-in-the-speculative-blank becomes its own news story, the media—intentionally or no—begins to fill the public psyche with a false sense of insecurity. Suddenly, air travel is perceived as dangerous. Conceivably, a family planning their vacation might decide to drive instead of fly—and thus increase their risk exponentially.

And *that* flies square in the face of public trust.

The Allegiant Turkey
Originally published in Airways News

"The evacuation resulted in several minor injuries, and—perhaps more to the point—bad publicity for the airline."

Nothing pisses off a line pilot more than a corporate stuffed suit sticking his nose in the safe operation of an airplane—especially when a proper, safe decision by the pilot results in his termination. In AirwaysMag.com's Thanksgiving "Turkey" awards for airline blunders, we awarded Allegiant Management a very deserving top spot.

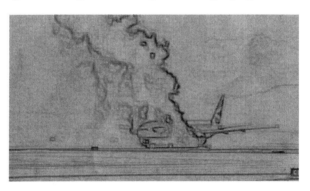

The job of Pilot-in-Command of an airliner is not an easy one. Sound decisions must be made, in real time, often with imperfect information, all while traveling at 8 miles a minute. And, if an accident or incident occurs on board, every microsecond will be scrutinized for years to come, not only by investigators, but by armchair pilots second-guessing every action or inaction. Those Monday morning quarterbacks can include the very company for whom those pilots work.

Such appears the case for Allegiant Air, who promptly fired Captain Jason Kinzer after what they claim to be an "unnecessary" evacuation after smoke was observed in the cabin. The evac resulted in several minor injuries, and—perhaps more to the point—bad publicity for the airline.

In June, 2015, smoke in the cabin initiated an emergency landing for Allegiant flight 864, which promptly diverted to St. Petersburg Clearwater International Airport.

Upon landing, a voice on the radio says, "I'm showing some smoke on your number one engine."

The pilot asks for confirmation. "Verify you're showing smoke on the number one engine?"

"That's affirmative. You wanna shut number one down. That's the pilot's side."

"Alright number one shutting down."

Shortly thereafter, the crew decides to evacuate. They report it over the radio. "Allegiant 864, we're gonna be evacuating."

"Allegiant 864, roger. And at that position, correct?"

"Yes, right here we're gonna be evacuating."

Soon after, another voice on the radio—presumably the fire crew chief—requests the crew to hold off. But, after multiple queries by the pilots, the voice is never confirmed, nor an explanation given as to why they should hold off.

"Allegiant 864, why do you want us to hold?" the crew can be heard transmitting. "Sir, we need an answer. Please, why do you want us to hold on the evacuation?"

Without further information, and with the smoke threat still presumably looming, the crew continues with the evacuation.

Smoke aboard an aircraft is nothing to be trifled with. Even if it turns out to be a minor issue, in seconds, that minor issue could flare into an onboard conflagration. Swissair 111, Air Canada 797, Value Jet 592… aviation history is rife with deadly examples.

With little data to go on, any flight crew would rightly divert and evacuate as soon as possible. It's simply the safest course of action. Captain Kinzer says he would do the exact thing all over again, and this pilot would do the same exact thing as well.

This incident is one of several that have plagued Allegiant Air. A report by the Aviation Mechanics' Coalition claims the airline had a "high rate of returns and diversions due to avoidable mechanical issues"—in all, 38 incidents between January and March of 2015.

Second-guessing a captain's split-second decision and going to the extreme length of termination sets a very dangerous precedent. The next captain facing a similar situation may hesitate, for fear of the same consequences—thus jeopardizing the lives of passengers and crew.

Captain Kinzer has filed a lawsuit against Allegiant for "Wrongful and Tortious Termination of Employment."

We believe he has a strong case, and wish him the best of luck.

Fly By Wifi? Think Again, Hacker!
Originally published in Airways News

Much ado has been made about Security researcher Chris Roberts allegedly hacking into wifi and "commandeering" a Boeing 737.

I believe it is much ado about nothing.

According to the original article in *Wired*, the FBI is quoted as saying: "(Roberts) stated that he thereby caused one of the airplane engines to climb resulting in a lateral or sideways movement of the plane during one of these flights," FBI Special Agent Mark Hurley wrote in his warrant application. "He also stated that he used Vortex software after comprising/ exploiting or 'hacking' the airplane's networks. He used the software to monitor traffic from the cockpit system."

I find all this highly doubtful.

In my opinion, *Wired* itself was too quick to laud one of its own, and jumped the gun on publishing the article before it properly researched the facts.

Today's most sophisticated aircraft are often referred to as "fly by wire." That term tends to elicit fear, sort of an aeronautical equivalent of Einsteins' exasperated comment about quantum entanglement: "spooky action at a distance." Since the Wright Brothers, however, traditional flight controls have always been, in a sense, "fly by wire." Pilots manipulated flight controls via wire cable from their joystick or yoke directly to control surfaces such as ailerons, elevator and rudder. With the advent of modern airliners, these controls got a turboboost from hydraulics lines.

One famous incident brought these hydraulic lines to the forefront, when, on July 19, 1989, United Flight 232 made a spectacular crash landing in Sioux City after the DC-10's Number 3 tail-mounted engine exploded, severing hydraulic lines. In an amazing feat of CRM and airmanship, Captain Al Haynes and crew saved the ship from complete disaster. While 111 people onboard perished, 185 survived.

The latest evolution in technology trades these heavy hydraulic lines for much-lighter electric wires—hence the term, "fly by wire." But they're still hardwired, directly from pilot controls to hydraulic servos right at the control surfaces. This saves gobs of weight, and thus allows for much more design redundancy—that is, back up wiring routed in different ways, in order to avoid another United 232 disaster.

Even today, the Boeing 737 Roberts allegedly hacked isn't even "fly-by-wire." The 737 remains built with good ol'-fashioned cables and hydraulic lines directly connected to flight control surfaces.

To hack anything, from a plane to a toaster, a perp needs one of two things: wifi to connect to another computer on the same wifi network, or a hard-wire connected directly to the target system.

In an excellent Op Ed explaining the story behind the headlines, NYCAviation Editor Phil Derner Jr and John Steffan say that Roberts' statement is equivalent to "your buddy claiming that he controlled your microwave by hacking into the TV's system."

In other words, other than sharing the same power source, the two systems are simply not connected.

Baloney, too, is Roberts' claim that he "caused one of the airplane engines to climb, resulting in a lateral or sideways movement."

As the two NYCA pilot-writers astutely point out, "Hacking into the flight control and engine management computers would require physically hacking through the floorboards and into the aircraft's E&E (electronic and equipment) compartment."

Cap'n Aux landing in KFLL. Photo courtesy Mark Lawrence.

In the NYCA article's Comment section, reader JimNtexas states, "This whole thing is nonsense. The guy pried open a seat and got on the inflight entertainment system (IFE) ethernet. There he saw these hosts: EICAS; PAX_OX_ON; SATCOM. Think of it as the debug output of the airplane. This clickbaiter just SAW these hosts, he wasn't able to effect anything on the airplane."

Similarly, one remote possibility may involve the ACARS (Aircraft Communications Addressing and Reporting System,) a digital datalink system for transmission of short messages between aircraft and ground stations via airband radio or satellite. Basically, it's email between pilots, dispatchers and maintenance. It also allows maintenance to monitor engine and aircraft system parameters to identify trends.

IF (and that's a big if) the onboard wifi is connected to ACARS, then perhaps its plausible one could muck with those readings. But again, just like JimNtexas' "debug outputs," these are merely readings, not commands.

Even so, scrambling ACARS data is a long way from actually connecting with an engine and causing it to "surge" and "fly sideways."

In an AirwaysMag.com Op Ed, John Walton is equally skeptical, likening it to a Boy who cried Wolf scenario: "It happens every year: conveniently prior to a major information security conference, a researcher claims to be able to hack a plane, and the general media demonstrates its negligence in aviation."

In his Forbes article, "US Government Claims Of Plane Wi-Fi Hacking Wrong And Irresponsible," staff writer Thomas Fox-Brewster says, "The information passed on to the inflight entertainment system is via something called a NED (Network Extension Device). This device is not a router. This is a one-way communication. Even if someone were able to send information back toward the avionics, they aren't listening."

While perhaps well-intentioned, Robert's biggest crime was endangering the plane with a potential onboard fire as he illegally fiddled with onboard electrical components. In this regard, he should be charged.

Let's leave the field testing to the pros, and not some whacker-hacker.

To be sure, this story should be used as a wake up call for the airline industry to be wary of future potential hazards. As planes become more tech-dependent and onboard IFE more tech-savvy, we need to ensure that never the twain shall meet.

Prince and . . . Chemtrails?

Originally published on Capnaux.com

"That friendly jet flying overhead is deliberately spewing out gobs of nasty chemicals. Why? To control your brain, of course!"

One of the most persistent and (ob)noxious aviation myths perpetuated by the conspiracy crowd is that of "chemtrails." According to them, some sinister world organization, such as the New World Order, (NWO), Triad or Illuminati secretly pays pilots to spew chemicals in the air to control the masses.

Strap on your tinfoil hats, boys, cuz Cap'n Aux is gonna dispel this myth once and for all!

It's been a tough year for music lovers, as in short succession we've lost no less than three icons: country legend Merle Haggard, androgynous rocker David Bowie, and now that even more androgynous rocker, Prince.

While I didn't really appreciate Prince's music back in The Day (do much more now), I've always greatly respected him as an artist. He passionately pursued his music through several instruments, and could and would fuse nearly any genre. He was also a passionate humanitarian, very busy behind the scenes, quietly helping others in many ways. For example, he was instrumental in creating the Yes We Code charity.

Prince always seemed to challenge our world view, and expand them in ways never done before—just as great artists always do. It really threw me, for example, when the little big man changed his name to that symbol thingy, prompting the media to address him as, "The Artist Formerly Known as Prince."

Cap'n Aux pumps out his quota of mind-controlling chemtrails.
Now, what was that secret Bahamas bank account number again?

He eventually changed his name back to just Prince—no doubt due to the fact that no computer keyboard in the world could type that symbol thingy—but by then the point was made. Basically, at least by my reckoning, his point was, Would a rose, by any other name, smell as sweet?

OK, that phrase was coined by the Bard in one of his most famous works, *Romeo and Juliet*, over 400 years ago. I mean, what he seemed to be saying to us is, What's in a name? Does my name, Eric, aka "Cap'n Aux," define me?

Sorry, gonna stop there; my brain hurts!

(By the way, the artist formerly known as that symbol thingy and currently known as Prince was the man born Rogers Nelson—may he rest in peace.)

OK, so if you have any inkling of interest in music, you probably already know most of what we were just talking about. But, did you know that Prince was murdered by chemtrails? It's 100% true!

At least, according to a few "truth-seeking" websites, he was.

What's a chemtrail, you ask? Well according to conspiracy nuts—uh, sorry, *theorists*—your friendly neighborhood jet flying overhead is not producing those pretty contrails by adhering to the most basic of physical processes (you know, that one about water vapor mixing in cold air to make that thing we call clouds?) Instead, they are deliberately spewing out gobs of nasty chemicals (and blatantly ignoring basic physics, to boot)!

Why?

Why, to control your brain, of course! And to cull the population.

Now, here's the real kicker: Prince *himself* believed in chemtrails.

I Photoshopped this pic a couple years back. As predicted, the chemtrail nuts have used it as "Proof." But I implore you: look very, very closely!

By his own reckoning and that of his fellow theorists, the sinister powers behind the thrones have for decades been dumping toxic purple rain on your little red corvette, to make both you *and* the doves cry.

What's more, according to some of his conspiratorial acolytes, our Seventh Day Adventist-turned-Jehova's Witness was prophetic as well, having predicted 9/11.

Well, the Triad/New World Order/Illuminati simply can't have psychic, prophetic musical geniuses running around tattling on its nefarious activities, now can it? Which leads us (apparently) to the . . . eh . . . "logical" conclusion that he was deliberately offed for "knowing too much." Again, according to some, Merle Haggard was summarily dispatched in the same way, for similar reasons.

But wait, there's more! According to the "truth-seekers," tens of thousands of us greedy, sinister pilot types are in on it as well, loading up each jet with the required doses for whatever population center needs to be controlled. Apparently, we all get hefty bonus checks for the double duty of doing the CIA's dirty work (or the Illuminati et al, depending on your choice of villain).

Sadly, after nearly 40 years of spraying—er, I mean, flying—the New World Order has yet to inform me of the number to my secret bank account in the Bahamas.

Friends, you can believe what you want about flat earths, fake moonshots, grassy knolls, and MH370. But I appeal to the tiniest smidgen of logic that I dare hope is still lurking in your frontal lobes by offering you this one, irrefutable and inconvenient truth:

What sane pilot would deliberately spray his/her own self, loved ones and progeny with mind-controlling chemicals?

If you *still* insist on believing in chemtrails, then I suggest you'd better double up your tinfoil helmets; I'll be doubling up my chemtrail load.

JOIN TEAM CHEMTRAIL!

Dip into that secret Bahamas bank account of yours and show your pride in being an evil sellout, controlling the masses and culling the herd!

Find this and other Kicka$$ Aviation Swag only at

cafepress.com/CapnAuxswag

100% of author "swag" proceeds goes to orphan charities!

The Airline Pilot's Kryptonite

Photo courtesy Jean Denis Marcellin, author, "The Pilot Factor."

"We have met the enemy . . . and he is us."—Pogo

This one was personal.

I've always striven to keep my airline's business out of my blog, books and writing. I do not represent them, but neither is it a secret for whom I work. Indeed, I am proud to be called a pilot for "the new American Airlines," the largest airline in the world.

However, I am not what you would call a "Native American." I came to it by way of the USAirways/American merger; and I came to *that* airline via the America West Airlines' buyout of bankrupt USAirways. FYI, I was hired by AWA in November 1990.

As anyone in the industry knows, airline mergers tend to be complete train wrecks, at least for the various employee groups. *Especially* the pilots.

When someone intentionally wrongs you in a particularly vindictive and callous way, you quietly take it like a victim, lash out blindly and ineffectually, or fight back properly. Well, my weapon of choice has always been words. When wielded properly, words can slice like a samurai sword, with the precision of a scalpel.

An article that has been nearly ten years in the making . . .

The image of the airline pilot is a super one.

Second only to firefighter, airline pilot consistently ranks as the top most-respected profession in the world. The stereotype of the stoic, benevolent, grandfatherly problem-solver in the sky is embedded in our psyche. Calm in the face of danger, the airline pilot gets 'er done. Plane on fire? No problem. Flock of geese fry your engines? On it. Cat caught in a tree? Keep calm and call an airline pilot.

But this heroic sky god has a secret weakness as powerful as Superman's Kryptonite, one that will reduce him to a blubbering, tantrum-throwing two year old. Worse, it threatens to transform the benevolent Supergramps into *Bizarro* Supergramps, a snarling, cannibalistic jackal willing eat his own kind.

This Kryptonite has a name: Seniority.

Seniority is everything to pilots. It dictates whether they're Captains or First Officers, hold a line (schedule) or are on reserve (on call), the size of the toy they get to fly, and in which city—from Paris to Pocatello—they're based. It determines whether they have weekends and Christmas off, or have to fly redeyes. It dictates whether they even *have* a job.

Unlike doctors, lawyers and other professionals, pilots cannot make lateral moves between companies. Why? Because seniority is nontransferable between companies. Besides, there is simply no easy measuring stick for saying, "This pilot is 'better' than that one, and therefore should be senior." Either a pilot can meet minimum flying standards, or can't. So, regardless of skill and experience, the pilot switching companies goes straight to the bottom of the next list (see, *What is a Co-pilot?* this volume).

As a result, for any given single company, seniority is solely based on date of hire (DOH). The longer a pilot stays—in theory—the higher up the food chain, and therefore the better one's schedule, pay, and job security. The more people beneath them, the more they are cushioned from furlough (layoff, with recall rights) during a downturn. When a single company is involved, everybody agrees: DOH is the only fair way to determine seniority. But when airlines merge, all hell breaks loose. Mergers unleash the pilot's kryptonite like Lex Luthor never could.

At first glance, DOH seems like a fair integration for any merger as well. What's good for the goose is good for the gander, right? Not necessarily. In some extreme cases, it can be devastating.

Regardless of the methodology used, however, no merged list is ever 100% "fair"—one pilot always moves up on the back of another. Moreover, "fair" is solely in the eye of the beholder. As a result, there has rarely been an airline merger wherein the pilots got together, held hands and sang *Kumbaya* while hammering out a reasonable, integrated seniority list. Instead, both sides often fight beak and claw for the slightest advantage, and will stop at nothing to press advantage. No dirty trick is forbidden.

There's no better example of this cannibalistic behavior than the 2005 purchase of bankrupt USAirways by the much younger, more nimble and financially sound company, America West Airlines.

At the time, original USAirways ("East") pilots had just about as many pilots on furlough (1,700, or 33% of the East pilot body) as America West ("West") had pilots. During seniority negotiations with ALPA (Airline Pilots Association, their mutual union), East pilots argued vehemently for DOH. This would have had the effect of "stapling" 80% of West pilots beneath the East (even below those that had been laid off), forcing the majority of West pilots onto the street—the very same pilots that had saved their jobs.

So much for singing *Kumbaya*.

During arbitration hearings, the West argued for a "relative seniority" integration, which would keep virtually all pilots—East and West—in their respective airplane, seat and base. This would have the added benefit of minimal costs for the new airline, by greatly reducing training required by the upheaval of pilots moving into different seats and equipment that DOH would have unleashed.

Arbitrator George Nicolau agreed to a relative seniority list, but placed 517 East pilots on top of the West pilots' entire seniority list. That is, the #1 West pilot was now #518. Every West pilot lost seniority, while every East pilot gained.

Fair? Again, fair is in the eye of the beholder. While the West pilots reluctantly agreed to the compromise (arbitration requires "agreement in advance"), the East pilots went, for lack of a better term, *bizarro*. Using their superior numbers (about two to one), the East forced the West out of ALPA and into their own, in-house union, "US Airways Pilots Association" (USAPA). USAPA's Prime Directive: implement their DOH list and ignore the legally binding Nicolau arbitration—even though they had agreed to the list in advance. What's more, the company had *already* accepted the Nicolau seniority list.

USAPA's very first act as a "union" (and we use this term loosely here) was to sue 24 West pilots—the very same pilots they claimed to represent— for the "crime" of fighting back. USAPA accused the 24 pilots of violating RICO laws, which had been designed solely to fight organized crime. What's worse, required by law to pay union dues, these alleged "Mafia" defendants were forced into the legally bizarre position of *suing themselves*. The suit was thrown out as frivolous, appealed, and thrown out again. But not without costing the 24 pilots tens of thousands of dollars in legal fees.

For the past ten years, more lawsuits have flown East and West like roundtrip transcons, with both sides fighting to a virtual stalemate. Only this summer, on the verge of the new merger with "native American" pilots, has the West finally managed a string of decisive legal victories, including a seat on the new seniority integration committee (all along, East pilots had *claimed* to represent West pilots), and a federal injunction requiring USAPA to advocate for the original Nicolau award. In typical fashion, upon being slapped with the injunction, East negotiators temporarily pulled out of negotiations.

By all accounts, USAPA failed as a union. Obsessed with DOH, it stonewalled all pilot contract negotiations. Once the top moneymakers, pre-AA-merger USAirways pilots languished at the rock bottom of the industry. And a work slowdown by USAPA hardliners—under the thinly-veiled guise of bogus safety concerns—was met with a blistering court injunction.

Nevertheless, USAPA's self-serving tactics have wrought the desired destruction. Its every action favored East pilots over West; something blatantly illegal under "duty of fair representation" (DFR) labor laws. Recent court rulings have confirmed these heinous acts. Luckily for the perps, a "Global Settlement" has been reached between East-West entities, avoiding fines and possibly even jail time for the guilty parties.

But the damage has been done. As a result of this schism, after the merger, dozens of active West pilots were subsequently furloughed, while all East furloughs were recalled, and hiring on the East began in earnest. To add insult to injury, with West pilots still on the street, these post-merger new-hire pilots on the East began *upgrading to Captain.*

No proper, upstanding union would ever allow such upside-down seniority without demanding that, at the very least, senior pilots stuck in lower positions receive equal pay as their junior captain counterparts.

USAPA's response? Silence.

While not nearly the debacle as AWA/USAirways, the recent mergers at United/Continental, Delta/Northwest and Southwest/AirTran have all experienced similar turbulence. And American Airlines' purchase of TWA was so volatile that it prompted Congress to create the McCaskill-Bond Amendment.

Three-way negotiations between East and West USAirways pilots and native American pilots have only recently begun. So far, with USAPA cronies muzzled and hamstrung by the recent court rulings, things appear to be moving forward. Moreover, the parties do seem to have taken lessons from the past as well, agreeing ahead of time to a three-person Federal arbitration panel to umpire the proceedings. But negotiations are barely past the introduction phase, and the nitty gritty work has yet to begin. Even so, a group of pilots has filed a lawsuit challenging the arbitration before the list has even been issued.

What stands to happen? If the past is any indicator, you'd better buckle your seat belts. As far as pilot seniority integration goes, we may be in for some serious self-inflicted turbulence.

In the immortal words of Pogo, We have met the enemy and he is us.

SECTION 5: The Cap'n Answers Your Q's

Have You Ever Had to . . .

One of the most consistently popular posts from my blog has been our "Ask the Cap'n" series, wherein readers wrote in with their own questions about life in the sky. While intended to be only one or two posts, the series blossomed into a six-part series, as droves of readers wrote in with great questions. I broke them down into different themes, beginning with this one. Here's the best of the best of our Q&A series!

— Have you ever had to Perform a go-around upon landing?

While not a daily occurrence, a go-around is very common, and is a standard procedure. On average, I have to perform one approximately every few months.

Basically, to abort the landing, you go from an approach mode, with gear and flaps down and flight-idle power, to climb out. Push the thrust levers to TOGA (Takeoff/Go-around), raise the gear and flaps, and circle around to try again.

If a plane is "shooting an instrument approach," such as an ILS, through the clouds, there's a point at which the pilots must land visually, or go-around. This is called a "Missed Approach."

Despite all the melodramatic, "I thought we wuz gonna die!" tales that passengers inevitably babble about to their friends afterwards, both maneuvers are totally routine. Personally, I would say we execute a go-around on average about once every six months. I talk about go arounds at the end of my video, *Zen and the Art of Landing* (vimeo.com/capnaux/zen).

The most common reason for a go-around is that the plane ahead has not cleared the runway fast enough. Other factors may be weather—a strong gust or rain squall obscures the runway, for instance. Or, we just don't like the approach for some reason—comin' in too hot, too high, etc.

Once in LAS, the winds were so gusty, the FO had to do three go-arounds! I took over and landed on the fourth try—barely. If we had not been able to land on that try, we would have diverted to LAX or PHX.

But again, go-arounds are totally routine.

—Abort a take-off?

While nowhere near as common as a go-around, a take-off abort is still somewhat routine. Like a go-around or engine failure, we practice them all the time in the sim.

In my career, I've only had to abort a takeoff once, in LAX, when a fuel valve went nuts and surged the Number 2 engine in our DeHavilland Dash 8. I gotta tell ya, those autobrakes during an abort are something else. I got plastered to the windshield! (And, by the way, our abort prompted the airplane behind us to go around—a bit of a domino effect!)

—Deal with a low-fuel situation?

Airline dispatchers are super good at figuring the proper amount of fuel.

Dispatchers are my friends! Really! See?

From time to time, I'll boost the fuel a bit if I feel the need. Knock on wood, in 22 years of flying for my airline, I've never had to cut into my emergency reserve fuel before landing.

The only time I "ran out of fuel" was as a student. For that story, see, *I Nearly Wet My Pants* in Volume I of this series.

—Handle an in-flight emergency?

Hey, that's what this whole *There I Wuz* series is about!

I've had a few in-flight emergencies over the years, but really nothing to write home about (only write books about)! As a flight instructor, I used to teach my students to "declare an emergency if you get a hangnail." You get priority ATC handling, and the fire trucks roll. It's always better to be safe than sorry.

Much along the same lines, I'll default to "declaring an emergency" when something's a bit suspect. Still, (again knock on wood), nothing news-worthy.

But the paperwork's a b*tch!

Even on a normal flight,
*the paperwork is a b*tch!*

—Handle an in-flight medical emergency?

A medical emergency is by far the most common emergency. We have a nationwide system called Medlink, where the pilots or flight attendants can patch in and talk to an MD. More than just pretty faces, flight attendants are also trained in basic medical procedures, including using the onboard defibrillator. Airlines have saved a few lives aboard over the years. However, if it involves breaking into the onboard emergency medical kit, it requires a qualified medic. On a typical airliner flight, there is often at least one doctor, nurse or EMT aboard, which helps immensely. If things get really dire, we may have to divert to the nearest suitable airport to get the patient on the ground and into a hospital, *stat*.

For more, see my article, *You're the Captain: Medical Emergency!*, the first story in Volume II of this series, and also published in the April, 2014 edition of *Airways* Magazine. It will put you in the driver's seat during an actual medical emergency and diversion I had—bring a hanky to wipe the sweat off your brow!

—Had to do an emergency descent because of pressurization issues – what are the procedures for that?

While it does happen from time to time, I've never experienced the real thing. However, we practice it in the sim quite often. It's one of the few "memory items" we have–basically, don our O2 masks, turn 90° off course (if on an airway), and dive. Followed up, of course, by the emergency checklist, declaring an emergency with ATC, landing at the nearest suitable airport, etc. For a fictional but accurate account, read, *Jihadi Hijacking*. See also, *Explosive Decompression*, the first story in Volume I of this series.

More common is a "slow depressurization.". Say, a door seal is not working that great, and the air pressurization can't keep up with it. So, slowly, the cabin altitude rises (i.e., the air pressure inside the plane decreases). This may result in the same thing—the oxygen mask "jungle" drops in the cabin, and we have to make a high dive to lower altitude—but again, it would be a relatively benign "emergency."

Run for your lives, it's a Haboob!
A Haboob (dust storm) encroaches on KPHX (Phoenix, Arizona). Haboobs frequently whip up the winds and lower visibility in the Phoenix Valley, which delays flights. A nuisance, but not hazardous.

—What is the worst storm situation you have dealt with?

Hmm, we deal with weather so much, that could be tough to answer. Hands down, however, would be my Hurricane Hugo adventure in the VirginsIslands, which I wrote about in Volumes I and II of this series (see, "Gone with the Hurricane," Part1 and 2).

99.9% of the time, severe weather means delay, avoidance and possibly diversion—that is, diverting to an alternate, circling, or simply sitting on the ramp or the gate until the storm passes. (By the way, weather RADAR is for thunderstorm *avoidance*, not *penetration*.)

My record wait time onboard a full plane was eight hours on the ramp in KEWR (Newark, NJ). That was the slowest moving storm front I ever saw, but there was nothing we could do about it. I simply kept the passengers informed the whole time, and to a one they were all nice and understanding. We were heading to Vegas, and one intrepid couple asked if, as the Captain, I could marry them (I wish I had said Yes—we certainly had time for it!)

I didn't mention to the passengers that, when we finally took off, it was within minutes of our "drop dead" legal maximum time to work. We nearly had to cancel the flight!

----
*Airplanes and hurricanes do NOT mix.
Believe me,
I know!*

—Can you vaguely talk about co-workers that you don't like working with?

Honestly, very few people come to mind with that question. By and large, "quirky personalities," shall we say, can be dealt with by treating that person with dignity and respect. Truly listening to what they have to say, and then validating their concerns. Most often, a conflict comes from lack of communication and understanding. Air disasters of the past have been studied for human factors, and we are now much more "evolved" and "enlightened" as to how to work with each other in the cockpit (See, *Top 5 Improvements in Modern Aviation Safety*, this volume.)

That said, the mark of a good FO (First Officer) is one who can almost psychically adapt to the quirks of the Captain's personality and still do his job. (Captains don't have that burden. My job is *much* easier in the left seat!) There's a lot of big egos in this business that are easily chafed.

Several times as an FO, I detected a potential conflict brewing. But, rather than getting upset and "tuning out," I found a way to validate the Captain's concerns. Suddenly, I was their best friend.

Needless to say, this concept works in everyday life as well.

—*Have you ever been aware of a mobile device being on or used in flight, and has it affected your systems?*

Yes. Like you, I was skeptical about the effects until, on one flight during Game 7 of the World Series, we noticed our instruments going a bit whacky. Turned out there were a dozen guys surreptitiously listening to their am radios, desperately trying to listen to the game. I had to make several announcements, finally scolding them over the PA into compliance. To compromise, we gave them frequent score updates.

Last year, I also had serious radio interference from several bobbleheads in back trying to use walkie talkies. There's a chance that they could actually have been, shall we say, *foreign agents* testing the systems.

While a receiving-only device such as an AM radio is not nearly as interfering as a transmission device like a cell phone, the bottom line is, there's not enough data to conclusively say how much any given device affects each type of airplane. So, to err on the side of safety, the FAA has made this blanket rule, at least for now. Yes, it's annoying, but can you imagine 100 people "accidentally" having their cell phones on at once?

—*Have you ever hit the wrong button leading to unintended consequences – e.g. the PA system?*

We have a saying in this business: "There's two types of pilots, those that have, and those that will." And yes, I am in the, "Those that have" category! There are good reasons we have two pilots up front. Humans make errors, and two heads are *wayyy* better than one.

Every few weeks, for example, we get to skewer yet another victim who unintentionally broadcast his PA over ATC frequency.

Once, instead of calling the Flight Attendant to ask for a pottie break, I almost broadcast over the cabin PA that I "had to use the little pilot's room.". Almost . . .

But I *did* tell ATC that once. Oh, man. You shoulda heard the comebacks on that one!

What's "Life on the Line" Like?

Part 2 of our Ask the Cap'n series dealt with the daily life of an airline pilot, and a typical "day at the office."

—What do you look for when you walk around the aircraft, prior to departure?

Our preflight inspection is fairly simple, logical and straightforward. Dings, dents, flat tires, and the like. Airline pilots can't even pull a panel—we need a mechanic for that. But, we do inspect our bird very closely.

In the cockpit, there's documents, safety equipment, avionics and computers to check as well. Anything amiss and we'll immediately call Maintenance.

Planes are machines, and as such subject to wear, tear and failures. Finding something is very common. But it's no big deal. Passengers are always worried that we're "pushing it," not "telling them everything," and compromising safety. What they fail to remember is, Hey, it's OUR butts on the planes too. (See, *Zen and the Art of Airline Maintenance*, Volume II of this series.)

—How often do you have to receive training? Simulator?

It depends on the airline and its procedures, but at my airline we do Recurrent training once a year. We have a day of Ground School, followed by two days of Simulator flying. Each sim session lasts four grueling hours, with the Captain typically flying the first two hours, and the First Officer the next two.

—How do you track the number of hours you have flown?

The only records I'm required to keep are the flights required to stay FAA-current. So, I let the Company do the record keeping. They have very accurate records, as required by the FAA. I'll print these up each month and that becomes my "logbook." I gave up on my own log book over 20 years ago.

I fly an average of 700 hours a year, so I have over 21,000 hours total time now. That's nearly 2-1/2 solid years spent in the sky! So at this point, does every minute really matter?

—What is a typical work week like?

It certainly ain't no 9-5 M-F gig. I typically fly a 3- or 4-day trip per week. Then, I'll normally have 3-4 days off. Sometimes, I'll have to fly up to the maximum of 6 days on/1 off. But, somewhere in there, I'll make up for it by having 1-2 full weeks off. And, after 25 years at my company, I am mostly able to avoid flying redeyes. By and large, a decent schedule.

Hey, it beats working for a living!

—What kind of vacation benefits do you receive?

Approximately four weeks per year. Normally, I'll try to space those weeks out across the year, or perhaps "float" the weeks and take them when needed, if it works for the company. You can usually expand a week of vacation into two or three if you wanna milk it right.

—Why is seniority so important?

Seniority is everything to an airline pilot. It dictates whether you're on reserve or have a schedule, if you have to work weekends, redeyes, and when you can upgrade to Captain. Sometimes, it dictates whether you even *have* a job.

That's why pilots fight so hard over it during mergers. (See, *The Airline Pilot's Kryptonite* in this volume.)

—How do you get your schedule ? I know you have to bid, but how – online, with a password ?

We use an online, computerized bidding system called PBS (Preferential Bidding System). Each month, we bid for our preferences—

whether or not to work weekends, nights, where we want to fly, etc. We can make it complicated or simple. Then, the computer builds our line for the month according to our preferences. The senior pilots get most or all of their preferences, the mid level pilots some, the junior pilots . . . eh, not so much.

Some airlines still bid the old way, by hand. They spend hours each month scouring over the pre-printed lines for the next month, and list their choices in order. Then, they are awarded whatever line they can hold according to their seniority.

After 25 years at my airline, I'm, well, mid-level or so in the left seat.

—Do you always do the same route, with the same person?

Almost never. In the old days, when we bid for whole lines by hand, we would fly with the same pilots and flight attendants for the whole month. But now, with the computerized PBS, it's far easier and more efficient. As a result, however, I'll normally fly with one FO for one trip, then a different FO for the next. We are always switching flight attendants from flight to flight, because they work under different rules now. Unfortunately, this prevents you from bonding with that crew for the month. On the other hand, you don't get stuck with that "quirky personality," either!

—Do you always fly in the same aircraft?

The same *type* of aircraft. At my Company, the A320 class Airbus fleet, which I fly, consists of A321, A320, or A319. I'll often fly all three in one trip, and hardly notice the difference. In fact, that's the philosophy of Airbus design—to minimize training events when transitioning between models.

—Do you prefer short or long flights?

My favorite trip is one that has only one or two legs per day, say a long and short one together like PHL-LAS-PHX. I don't like a high number of legs, as one little delay can create a domino effect, and suddenly your 8-10 hour day becomes 12 or 14. Then again, your delayed flight may cancel your next one (that is, Scheduling will substitute a standby crew in your place), and you get off the trip early. To "pray" for this early release, crews will do a little jig called "the cancel dance!"

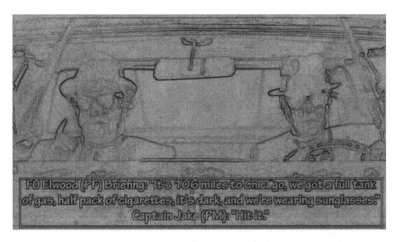

FO Elwood (PF) briefing: "It's 106 miles to Chicago, we got a full tank of gas, half pack of cigarettes, it's dark, and we're wearing sunglasses." Captain Jake (PM): "Hit it."

—So the Pilot Flying (PF) briefs the the Pilot Monitoring (PM) before the flight. What does he/she talk about?

Basically, you're describing how you expect the flight to depart, from taxi out through climb. You'll review the weather conditions, what's on the MEL (Minimum Equipment List of inop items, if any) and how that will effect takeoff performance; your ATC clearance and how it may differ from the original flight plan. You'll also brief what you'll do if, say, you lose an engine on takeoff. You'll review the airport diagram and the route to your runway, noting any "hot spots" where runway incursions could occur, review the SID (Standard Instrument Departure) you're on. That way, both pilots are on the same page and ready in case of issues.

For landing, you'll do a similar briefing, reviewing the STAR (Standard Terminal Arrival Route), instrument approach, runway, landing performance, and taxi-in.

—I know if you encounter windshear ahead on an approach, the procedure is an automatic go around. But what if the windshear isn't detected in time and you end up flying into it?

Windshear has been a very serious threat to airliners and other aircraft. Since the loss of Delta Flight 191 in Texas in 1985, many studies and improvements have been made to detect and avoid windshear, such as the LLWAS (Low Level Windshear Alert System) around most major airports.

If you actually encounter windshear on takeoff or landing, the escape requires *no* configuration change, but instead a full power/max climb out, keeping the gear and flaps in their original position. You don't want the increased drag of gear doors opening, nor loss of lift with a flap retract. In the Airbus, if windshear is suspected, we'll use Flaps 3 for landing rather than full, for better maneuverability.

—How do you balance the need for the flight attendants to do their job, versus, the need for them to "sit down?"

Excellent Question. Part of their job *is* sitting down. In fact, it's the best place for them. Passengers see them as nothing more than waiters and waitresses in the sky, but that's *not* why they're in the plane. They are an integral part of the safety team.

In rough weather, and for takeoff and landing, they need to be at their stations—i.e., jumpseat, evenly spaced throughout the cabin, to deal with emergencies. In an evacuation, they will be properly positioned to deploy the slides, if need be.

Mostly, I need to eyeball the weather ahead, listen to other aircraft ride reports, etc. If something looks iffy, I'll order them back in their seats. As always in this biz, it's better to be safe than sorry.

—Would you discuss Captain's Emergency Authority?

Good question. Basically, it's the Captain, or "Pilot in Command," that needs to make sure the airplane is being operated safely and within FAA regulations at all times. If an emergency arises, however, the pilots are exempted from Regulations, as necessary, to meet the needs of that emergency.

FAR (Federal Aviation Regulation) 91.3 states:

Title 14 CFR 91.3: Responsibility and authority of the pilot in command.
(a) The pilot in command of an aircraft is directly responsible for, and is the final authority as to, the operation of that aircraft.
In an in-flight emergency requiring immediate action, the pilot in command may deviate from any rule of this part to the extent required to meet that emergency.

Is it legal, for example, to land an Airbus A320 in the Hudson River? If you did it for kicks, they'd lock you up and throw away the key. But shuck two engines in a sky full of Canadian geese, and I'd say the FAA wouldn't complain too much. Do it right, and you might even get a lucrative book deal and movie made of ya.

—*What are your responsibilities, when you are <u>not</u> the pilot?*

Another good question. To clarify, there are two pilots aboard the modern airliner, a Captain and a First Officer (FO). (We won't go into International Relief Officers, Flight Engineers, etc.). Both are FULLY qualified pilots (See, *What is a Co-Pilot?* in this Volume.) One has more seniority, and is therefore in the left seat, the Captain's seat. Both work together as a team, but ultimately the Captain is the final authority to, and is fully responsible for, the safety of the airliner.

As for flying, Captains and FOs trade off flying duties from leg to leg. The pilot driving the plane is known as the PF, or "Pilot Flying."

The "Pilot Monitoring," or PM, handles everything but the operation of the airplane itself. He/she answers the radios, gets the weather, makes the PA, communicates with the Flight Attendants. The PM basically does anything NOT involved with directly flying the plane.

—*What are your responsibilities, when you are the pilot?*

Again, the "Pilot Flying," or PF, flies the plane. Period. Under normal circumstances, that's the PF's *sole* job. If anything whatsoever happens, first and foremost, the PRIME DIRECTIVE is FLY THE PLANE!

Secondly, both PF and the PM should always know where they are and where they're going. This sounds silly, but planes have been lost due to simple disorientation.

Back to the "Prime Directive." If I, as the PF and Captain, need to handle something else, a "non-normal" or emergency, I will FIRST positively transfer control of the flying duties to the FO. Only THEN can I address the other issue.

We learned this most basic tenet when we lost United 173 in 1978. With the crew preoccupied with an improper landing gear indication, the plane ran out of fuel and crashed in Portland, killing 10 of 189 onboard.

Sadly, we should have learned this harsh lesson six years earlier, when we lost Eastern Air Lines 401 in 1972. The crew became so preoccupied with diagnosing a problem that all three pilots failed to notice the autopilot had kicked off and was descending. It crashed, killing 101 of 176 onboard.

All because of . . . a burned out light bulb.

What's the MCDU Cost Index? & Other Techie Q's

Now things get more technical. What are the gizmos aboard your plane, and what do you do with them? Strap in, this will be pretty heavy duty. But also delightful, if you're a certified avgeek.

—What is the fuel burn-rate of your aircraft? Taxi? Cruise? Climb?

You can Google the tech manuals and find all that stuff, so I'll give you my personal Rules of Thumb, gleaned over my 20+ years in Fifi.

First of all, "miles per gallon" doesn't work in an airplane. Fuel is a volatile gas, and temperature and pressure affect the volume. So, we use weight, in pounds (1 gal. = 6.4-6.8 lbs.) Secondly, our speed over the ground is dependent on winds, just like a boat in a river is affected by current. So, we use "pounds per hour" burned.

In short, we burn about 4-6,000 lbs per hour at cruise, depending on altitude and load. Conservatively, that's about 100 lbs per minute. This makes it very easy to determine how many minutes you have for a given fuel load.

The most common time we'll use this estimate is when we have to enter holding and need to know how long we can hold before having to divert to our alternate airport.

For taxi, we'll burn between 300-800 lbs, depending on how much traffic, taxi time, etc.

—Do you have to use both left / right hands on the control stick, based on where you sit?

In the Airbus, if you're a First Officer, i.e., flying from the right seat, you fly the joystick with your right hand. Captains, in the left seat, use their left hand. I like to joke that, being left handed, I'm a "Born Captain."

You may think it would be strange flying with the "wrong hand," like writing with your opposite hand. But it takes all of five minutes to get used to it.

—Is your route determined by the Dispatcher? What are the factors?

The Dispatcher's computer will factor in all the data, including predicted winds aloft, weather, and traffic flow, to come up with an ideal route and altitude. Often we will step up or down in Flight Levels to take advantage of winds as well.

Often, our "best route" is a mighty circuitous one. That is, if we go the Great Circle Route, i.e., "straight to destination," we'll burn MORE gas and take LONGER to get there, due to strong headwinds or weather deviations.

—How is an aircraft balanced when it is loaded? What does the Loadmaster do?

Weight and Balance loading is critical, even in large airliners.

Like ships on the sea, they have to be balanced properly and not overloaded. We have a "Loadmaster" who collates all the data—passengers, cargo, fuel, etc. That is then loaded into a sophisticated W&B computer to determine proper loading.

On some military aircraft, especially cargo carriers, the Loadmaster actually flies onboard as part of the crew.

We receive the "Numbers" on taxi out, and have to load the data into the onboard computer so it can properly assess actual weight, fuel burn, etc. If you're ever on a plane or listening to Tower on liveatc.net, and a pilot says they're "waiting for the numbers," that's what they mean.

I never felt like a real airline pilot until I had to inform ATC that I was "Waiting for the numbers!"

—What is the Cost Index, and how do you use it?

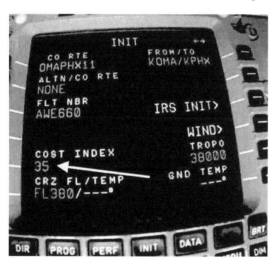

The Cost Index is a pretty cool feature.

First, a quick lesson: the faster a jetliner goes, the more fuel it burns. And we're talking hundreds, if not thousands, of gallons. That's the reason, when you're late, the Captain may elect to *not* put the pedal to the metal to make up for it. Tons more fuel burned, for only a few minutes made up—and he may need to hold that extra fuel in reserve for potential weather deviations, traffic holds, etc.

You can enter a number between 0 (slowest) and 99 (fastest, usually M.80 or so at cruise altitude). Typically, a number around 25-45 gives a decent average fuel savings and speed. If ahead of schedule, the Company may have the pilots input a cost index of 10, which slows the plane back. The flight still arrives on time or early, but saves gobs more fuel. (At any time, however, the pilot can select any speed desired, or as assigned by ATC.)

99 is the highest practical number you can enter, which gives the fastest speed (usually M.80 or so). These days, a number around 35 gives a decent average fuel savings and speed. If ahead of schedule, the Company may have the pilots input a cost index of 10, which slows the plane back. The flight still arrives on time or early, but saves gobs more fuel.

—On take off, you advance to 50% till stabilized, then set FLEX (Flexible temp, or Reduced Thrust) or TOGA (takeoff/go around thrust) detent. I seem to remember reading that the engines have a dead zone where you have to power straight through.

You might be mixing up the start sequence with the power up sequence. During start, the older model IAE-A1 engines were found to have a "harmonic zone" where the fan blades would receive excessive fatigue, and wear out early, so extra time was needed during the spin-up to ultimately power through that dead zone. Later models addressed this via the ECU (Engine Fuel & Control Unit, which would keep the power out of this zone).

As for takeoff, it is somewhat standard practice to power up to about 50% N1 for a couple seconds before cobbing it to takeoff power. While some engines may need this practice to avoid their own dead zone, the main reason is to avoid the engines spooling up unevenly, giving the pilot a bit of a zigzag ride down the runway. Coincidentally, on the Airbus, we pause somewhere around the "T", as in "Thrust," on the "A/THR" notation on the levers.

—Upon rollout after landing, how do you deactivate the autobrakes? Is it by tapping the toe brakes?

Right on the money, my friend.

—Hey Capn Aux, I'm just wondering what does the "TO SHIFT" on the Take Off page of the MCDU mean, and what is it used for?

When you throttle up on the runway for takeoff, the MCDU updates our position to the IRS system, knowing we are taking off at the end of the programmed runway.

If we take off from an intersection, however, we need to tell the box how far away we are from that. With the addition of GPS, this method is somewhat obsolete.

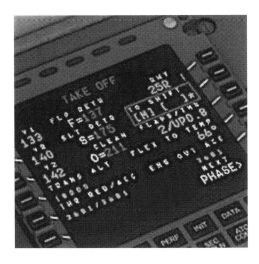

Blog Buddy-submitted pic of the TO Shift, from a flight sim program.

—*So, in my example above, if I took of from Intersection A3, I would enter the distance from that point to the RWY25R point?*
Correct.

You'll find the distance data on the Airport Diagram. A3 Intersection takeoff.

Performance must be calculated to ensure a safe takeoff from this intersection, and the MCDU must be told the "TO SHIFT"—ie, distance from the runway end to A3, in order to update the IRS as to the aircraft's position.

If you forget to plug it in on a non-GPS aircraft, there will be a bit of a "bias" error built in to the NAV data, but the constant updating from VOR triangulation will eliminate the bias error pretty quickly, so it normally wouldn't be a major issue.

Another Blog Buddy-submitted pic of the TO Shift depicted on an airport diagram.

LAS VEGAS/McCARRAN INTL (LAS)
LAS VEGAS, NEVADA

—*Once you are cleared for a visual approach to a runway, can you still do an ILS (Instrument Landing System)?*

Yes. Think of an ILS as a straight-in approach. During an actual ILS, you would be vectored to the final, straight in ILS approach somewhere

OUTSIDE the FAF (Final Approach Fix, 5-7 miles from the runway). The FAF is also about where you will intercept the glideslope of an ILS. The ILS glideslope is about the same descent path you'd use, regardless of whether on instruments or visual.

Either way, flying visually or doing the official ILS, the easiest thing to do is arm the ILS approach to intercept, and fly the course and track to the runway. So, while you're flying visually, you can still "back it up" with the ILS. It's just good practice to keep you more aligned for a good landing.

Operationally, being cleared for a visual or an ILS are virtually the same thing. In either case, ATC is vectoring you to intercept the final approach course on a specific heading, usually within 30 degrees of final. If you are cleared for a Visual approach, however, the rules are much more relaxed for aircraft clearance.

—Also, is it possible to do a visual with Autopilot? Or only flying by hand?

You can hand fly a visual approach or an ILS (CAT I; CAT II/III require autopilot), or you can fly an ILS or visual approach on the autopilot. Either way is fine—pilot's choice.

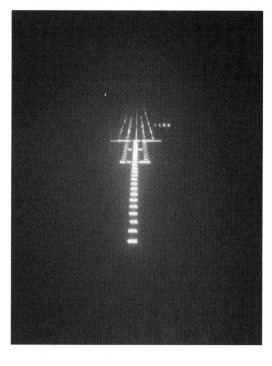

Approach lights in sight after shooting the ILS—and then transitioning to a visual, as is necessary to land during a CAT I approach.
Note the PAPI on the right indicating "on glidepath."

What may be confusing you is that, once you call the field "in sight," ATC can clear you for a visual approach w/in 30 miles of the airport. So, you could be on a downwind, base, whatever, when you are cleared. So, it's up to you to turn however you want. But, eventually, you're going to end up on Final, on a straight-in approach to the runway, five miles or so out. The ILS localizer course will be exactly on this track as well, so it's easiest just to fly yourself to an intercept course then arm the localizer/ILS button to intercept.

Most pilots "kick off" the autopilot on short final and land by hand. Otherwise, the autopilot can do an "Autoland.". But, certain parameters have to be met regarding operational equipment on the plane and on the ground for an autoland to take place.

—What are the procedures involved in a diversion, specifically how you update the MCDU? Are you cleared to a waypoint or fix by ATC and then build the plan from that point? Do you delete the existing plan and build a new one?

We type the Alternate into the INIT page before the flight, to estimate the fuel needed and keep an eye on the extra.

If we actually need to divert, we will "Line Select" a random waypoint from the left side. On the page that pops up, we can type in a "New Dest," say, "KDEN" (Denver Int'l). From there, we manually build the flight plan back in.

Most often, ATC will vector us to a waypoint along that route.

—What is your typical Fuel On Board on arrival–I'm guessing a couple of thousand kilos?–(or do you work in lbs–remember the Gimli Glider!)

Haha, thanks for reminding me of the Gimli Glider!

(Wiki: http://en.wikipedia.org/wiki/Gimli_Glider)

Standard arrival for our fleet of A320-class is around 5,000 lb, which gives us around an hour of fuel. Get much below that, and we start getting nervous. (FAA minimum is 45' of fuel.)

Several related Q's about taxiing and turning

—How do pilots know how to time turns when taxiing? How do they know when to make that turn to get ready for takeoff?

Good Q. Not really sure of an answer, other than you learn to "eyeball" it, much like you would learn how to drive. We fly the plane so much, it becomes second nature. Even so, we all err a little bit here and there, so hopefully we have some fudge factor.

—At what sort of speed can you take the hi-speed exit off the runway?

We are never watching the "speedometer" (airspeed indicator) at that point because it's irrelevant. I'm guessing somewhere around 40-50 kts, but we are still romping on the brakes pretty good at that point.

By the time we turn onto the taxiway, we are down to horse n buggy speed (a little aviation trivia: the first Federal Aviation Regulations, circa 1920's, called for a taxi speed of "no more than a brisk walk.")

—I play a lot of flight simulators. When I'm on the ground taxiing, I have struggled doing turns at 30mph, so I wondered, what is the taxiing speed and is it hard to turn while around 30-40mph?

Wow, you go, Speedracer! Our max taxi speed STRAIGHT AHEAD is 30. To turn, we're down around 10-15 max.

—How do you "cold start" your aircraft?
Eh...a slightly complicated question . . .

If we step aboard a "cold, dark" airplane, there's a checklist we go through to get ground power going. Basically: park brake verified set; engine masters off; landing gear handle verified down. (Even though the plane should "know" it's on the ground and won't raise the gear when we turn the power on, I ain't gonna be the first pilot to test it!)

Now, we select the ground power on (overhead). When we push the switch, it changes from the green "Avail" light to a blue "On." Now the plane is powered and the lights come on. We'll push the Battery 1 & 2 switches on, so they'll receive charging, and will be a backup if the External drops offline.

Once the CRT's warm up, we can actually see the power system on the ELEC page, if we select it on the lower ECAM. AC Busses 1 & 2, TR (Transformer/Rectifiers) 1&2, DC and AC Essential, and DC Battery Busses should all powered.

From here, we'd eventually turn on the APU (Auxiliary Power Unit), which is basically a small jet engine in the tail. The APU could actually be used as an engine on a turboprop. Once the power is switched over, we can have the ground crew disconnect Ext.

For airflow through the cabin, we'll also select APU bleed air on. Now the APU supplies electrical power and air. That's the noisy whine you hear when boarding a plane: the air conditioning "Packs" that blow air through the cabin.

Usually during pushback, the ground crew will clear us to start.

Now we get to your question

Starting a motor on an airbus is easy. Once cleared, we simply switch the Engine Ignition switch to "Start," and flip the desired Engine Master switch up and On. The computer does the rest.

If there's a problem, the computer will shut the engine back down. In that case, we'll probably have to call maintenance. In some cases, we can start it "Manually," which is a

similar process, but we manually open and close the Start Valves and monitor the start parameters ourselves (getting enough air flow to spin up, not getting too hot, no "hung starts," etc).

—How do you memorize the overhead panel?

"When eating an elephant take one bite at a time."—General Creighton Abrams

Just like anything, we have to learn…slowly.

However, "memorize" might be a bit misleading. You couldn't blindfold me, for instance, and ask me to hit the Bus Tie switch. But, just like fiddling with your car radio while driving, things you use every day become second nature. I can always reach up and hit the taxi light, the rotating beacon or the windshield wiper without ever looking for them, because I'm always using them.

While I couldn't sketch out every button on the overhead panel from memory, I could sketch you schematics for the Electrical, Hydraulic, Fuel or Pressurization systems. Those we learn thoroughly in ground school (again, one bite at a time). I may not be as sharp as I once was at nailing every circuit and buss on the Electrical in my sketch, but that training, along with working the systems for years, have given me a thorough "working knowledge" to deal with them.

Also, the shapes of many switches are designed differently from each other, so you can recognize them by feel. But, when a mechanic replaces a Taxi light toggle switch with a Beacon light paddle switch . . . man, that really throws you off.

—Do you have to fly Airbuses of a certain age? I am sure there is differences between old and new (CRT vs LCD, upgrades, etc)?

No. The Airbus was designed specifically for minimal cross training. Even between the 319-321's, we hardly notice the difference.

The Boeing-737, having started production much earlier, didn't originally have that concept, but does now. Even so, one type rating covers all B-737s, even though a pilot would need a little "differences" training, especially going from the "hard ball" to the EFIS, or glass cockpit. Nearly every B-737 cockpit out there is different in little ways, which annoys the 737 driver to no end. The Airbus…nary a diff.

—On the sim on which I "play", the 320 series never seems anywhere close to the "Coffin Corner." Is that correct, and have you ever flown with the barber poles converging?

> Note: "Coffin Corner" = max and min flying speeds converge.
> "Barber poles refer to the minimum and maximum speed lines
> on the airspeed tape.

The MCDU computer gives us our ideal cruise and max cruise altitude on the PROG page. We don't go above the "max," which has a built-in fudge on Coffin Corner, by, I'd say, at least about +/- 7-10 kts or so.

—What are the different radios, nav & communications you use?

Airbus radios are, shall we say, a bit "over-engineered."

First of all, we have the RMP, or Radio Management Panel. With this, we can manually tune ATC radio frequencies. We can also manually tune VORs, ILSs, etc. (all NAVAIDS), but this is mostly done automatically, and we would be using the manual feature as a backup.

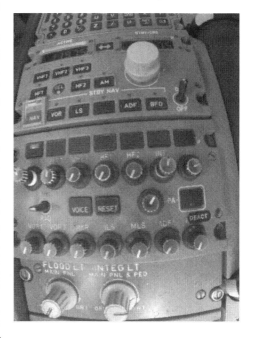

Once we dial in the freq. on the RMP, we transmit and receive by selecting the ACP, or Audio Control Panel. With it, we can select to listen and talk with ATC (or other entities such as Company or Emergency "Guard" on 121.50) on 3 different radios, talk to the flight attendants, the ground crew if at the gate, or even the PA.

Currently, we have three of each of these units; one for the Captain, one for the FO, and one as a standby. We normally use the #1 frequency for ATC, and #2 for calling Company, monitoring Guard, etc. Each of these are interconnected and can be used to substitute for the other.

NAVAID-wise, we have GPS, IRS, VOR, RNAV, ILS, ADF . . . you name it.

Combo Q from several readers: What are waypoints? How do you guys know how to pronounce these waypoints? And at these waypoints on the ground, are there those red towers? I have one near my house.

Waypoints are imaginary points on the ground. There are millions of them established around the world. Many come from actual points, such as VOR (VHF Omni Range radio beacons) broadcast stations on the ground. But, they don't need red towers, they can be completely imaginary. With today's technology, we can put a waypoint anywhere. So, instead of zigzagging across the country, hopping from one VOR to another, we can draw a much "straighter" line to follow, saving tons of gas and time.

We can even "build" our own waypoint in the computer. We can establish a waypoint several ways, such as a place/bearing distance from an established point (again such as a VOR), or even use raw Lat/Long data.

On arrival into SFO, I always build a waypoint over top of my family's traditional secret camping spot in the Sierra Nevadas—we've been packing in there since the 1940's. During the arrival, the waypoint on my screen helps me to find the spot.

"Little highways" is an apt description. We will be planned on those routes, but if the traffic is clear, ATC often gives us shortcuts. All SIDs (Standard Instrument Departures) STARs (Standard Terminal Arrival Routes), and instrument approaches have waypoints, each with its own specific name. They are often named for the area they are by, like a town or a lake or something.

We have to guess at how to pronounce some of these names. For example, we have the "Geela 6 Arrival" into PHX—everyone says hard G as in "guitar," but the original pronunciation of "Gila," (as in, Gila monster) is "Hee-la."

As a PHX native, it drives me crazy to hear it mispronounced.

Sometimes even the FAA gets creative with the names. I remember one arrival into PHX, long defunct, that had the waypoint names "DARF," followed by "VADRR," and my personal favorite, "FUBAR.". Going into KMCI, we have "SPICY," "BARBQ" & "RIBBS."

And, apparently KPHX has lots of sports fans: On the Bunter 2 Arrival, we have HOMRR, BUNTR & PICHR. On the Maer 5, we have FBALL, KARDS, PGSKN and TLMAN, named after our Arizona Cardinals football hero, Pat Tillman, who left the NFL to join the Army Rangers after 9/11.

He was killed in action in Afghanistan.

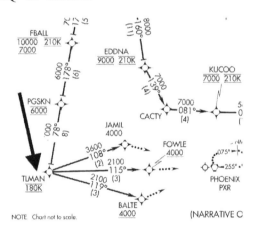

This article is dedicated to the memory of Pat Tillman.

Pot Pourri of Q's

—I know you like to carry a paintbrush to clean the panels, what other little rituals or habits have you observed amongst your fellow pilots in your time at the pointy end? Anything weird or interesting?

You know me too well!

All Captains seem to have their own personal quirks, some benign, some majorly annoying. There's a high percentage of Captains, for example, who just *love* that PA. They either think themselves tour guides, or stand up comics. My buddy Cap'n Tony is a born comic, and I love his PA's. Sadly,  however, most Captains need to "not quit their day job." It can drive the passengers—and especially the flight attendants—nuts!

As far as I know, my "biggest quirk" is that I am always tweaking the brightness of the lights in the cockpit. I guess I'm sensitive to that, so as the sun sets I am always dimming them down. Some, eh, elder pilots don't always see so well at night, so they tend to fight me, turning them back up.

—What is the typical length of time for a flight crew from walking down the jetway to ready for pushback? Presumably it depends what state you take over the aircraft in?

We are required to be at our ships around 40 minutes prior to departure, but normally we can get ready in half that time. It takes all of 10' for us to review the safety gear, check the paperwork, and preflight the plane. But, if there's a glitch—say, extra fuel is needed or maintenance required—we need to be there early enough to try and get 'er done to avoid taking a delay.

For international flights, we'll need a little extra time to maneuver through Customs and such. Recently, we had to deal with three countries in one day—Mexico, USA, and Canada.

—A lot of paperwork is generated for every flight – how long does it take to review and digest that paperwork and the weather for the routing – and how often is it necessary to contact the dispatchers for changes due to weather during the flight.

Yep, there's a lot of paperwork.

I can review the paperwork (called the "Dispatch Release") fairly quickly...about 5-10 minutes or so. 95% of the time, it's a no-brainer— no significant weather or other factors. The Dispatchers do an outstanding job of planning each flight, with the help of excellent flight planning software. So, mostly I am "reviewing their homework."

Have I mentioned yet that the paperwork is a b*tch?

The flights are often planned several hours in advance, however, so if things such as the weather change, I can always contact the Dispatcher and add more fuel. This happens only about 1 out of 10 flights.

The tough part is searching through a virtual encyclopedia of NOTAMS (Notices to Airmen) about the airports, etc. These are the latest notes issued by the FAA about taxiway closures, construction on the field, NAVAIDS down, etc. Also important are SIGMETS (SIGnificant METeorological info). about weather hazards and such. It can be a virtual search for a needle in the haystack, however, as nearly all of the stuff doesn't even apply to us. But, occasionally, we'll spot one that affects our flight, say a runway closure at ORD, or a line of weather developing over OMA, and we have to plan accordingly.

—Do airlines look for hours or a flight diploma or some sort?

In the United States, to get in the door, you need a college degree, preferably a 4-year degree. After that, flight hours. This is by far the biggest factor in hiring. Today, all 121 pilots are required to have an ATPL—Airline

Transport Pilot License. This requires a minimum of 1,500 hours (with some exceptions), although most pilots hired by a 121 carrier have much more flight time than that.

I've also found that having a "colorful history" helps. I was interviewed by my airline's pilot hiring committee just to hear about my experience flying the Alaskan bush, and for the Virgin Islands Seaplane Shuttle during Hurricane Hugo. It got me a foot in the door, and ultimately the job.

—How common is it for wannabe pilots to start life as a Flight Attendant?

Fairly common, actually. I've known about a half dozen or so, of which two or three have made it so far. Merely anecdotal evidence here, but it does seem to crack open the door for them. It's a bit of a double edged sword, however, because you are betting the farm that that particular airline will hire you . . . and you'll not be able to run around the world, building time at different outfits, if you're tied down to your flight attendant job.

Besides, the pay is lousy. How the $*^&^%#@ are you going to pay for your lessons?

—How often do the Passengers send gifts to the cockpit and what is your favourite gift to receive?

Geez, I'm on the wrong flights . . . almost never!

OK, once in a rare while we receive a chocolate or something. That's about it. I DO love giving out wings to the kids who visit. It is just what I live for!

Sweet little darling Destiny hand-wrote a poem for each member of the crew, and gave us each a box of candies to boot. Needless to say, in gratitude I gave Destiny a signed copy of one of my books!

An iPad Mini might be a nice gift for the flight deck . . .

—How much consideration do you give to your health before flying? For instance, I would have no problem going to work with a heavy cold, but at which point would you call in sick?

A pilot has to be 100%, period. If there's an accident or incident, the first thing the FAA will say is, "What? You were sick and you flew? *Violation!*" So, if I'm feeling something coming on, I probably won't hesitate to call in sick. I think, frankly, I owe it to the passengers to give them a flight crew operating at maximum health.

It is a continual challenge keeping healthy on the road. Getting good rest is a particular challenge, as we're often sleeping through the day, or next door to the hotel party. I always kick on the hotel room fan for a little white noise to muffle out sounds, and sleep with earplugs and an eye mask. With those, I'll still be able to hear my alarm.

The toughest challenge of all is having a report time the next day that's, say, 3am body clock time. That means forcing yourself to sleep at around 6 or 7 pm your time. Gotta pop some Tylenol PM's in that case . . . .

—I'm interested to know how a typical day pans out for you, in terms of how you find the time for writing, blogging, pubbing etc. – seems a full schedule – how do you relax (clean answers only plz!)

Hmm, "only clean answers"—a challenge!

In the cockpit, by some strict interpretations of FAR's (read: lawyers), the pilots are not allowed to do anything but stare out the window. But, the brain must stay engaged in order to keep sharp, so a pilot may—eh, in theory—read the paper, do a crossword or sudoku, etc, lest they get fatigued by boredom.

Blogging and writing has taken up a big chunk of my free time (just ask my poor, dust-covered banjo and guitar), so I do most of my writing and blogging during down time in hotel rooms.

At home, I spend time with my girlfriend, cats, friends and golf clubs. I make sure to get a workout in every day, also. My gal is a competitive body builder (she recently took first in the regionals, which qualified her for this year's nationals), so I gotta keep up.

—Hi, a question regarding something you noted in the readers' questions. You said that you fly about 700 hours a year. But isn't it true that commercial pilots can fly up to 100 hours a month? If so, why are your annual hours not closer to 1200? Is there a minimum per month that you have to fly/work?

(Note: The new FAR 117 has changed this answer slightly, but it is easier to explain via the old rules.)

For Part 121 airline flying, our max allowed flight time is approx. 100 flight hours/month. Believe me, if you're close to that, you're tired. 1,000 is also the max per year, so if you're flying the max each month, you're gonna "time out" and have the last two months of the year off. (This is actually how some people try to get Christmas off!)

Airlines build average lines for their pilots in a range of 65-85 hours (each airline is different). You can usually pick up extra time, or drop down lower to a minimum amount. My actual flown hours each month is usually around 60-80, but I typically get paid a higher range of "credit" hours. (Paid for deadheading, canceled flights, training, etc.)

Our duty hours—that is, our time at the airport at work, is easily twice our actual time flown. But most airlines base pay on flight hours, not duty time. That is why airline pilot hourly rates look so crazy-high. You may get paid for four hours of flying, but you work twelve hours to get it.

—What's your favorite airport to land at?

Probably DCA if we're doing the River Visual to 18, or JFK, if we're doing the VOR or visual to 13L. Maybe BUR as well. Those're about the only really "challenging" approaches left in our system. Not "hazardous" per se, but you have to pay attention. PVR (Puerta Vallarta), cuz that's my favorite overnight. TEX (Telluride, CO), is one of my old favs', too, not only for the challenge, but also because it means I'm going skiing, or to the Telluride Bluegrass Festival.

—How do you know what hotel you'll be at on an overnight? Do you pay for it?

That is planned months in advance, and all our hotels are booked and paid for by the Company. When we pull into an overnight city, we merely have to walk out of the airport curbside to the hotel van, which (we hope) is already waiting for the crew to whisk us to our—eh, hopefully decent accommodations. If we're traveling on our own, we can sometimes get nice discounts at hotels that we would stay in when we're working.

—Let's say you have a week off. Can you go to Paris or another country in that week off for free or it has to be during your vacations?

Absolutely. Many people get into the airline biz for one reason: to travel. But not for free. We buy "ID90's" or "ZED fares"—basically hugely discounted tickets on whatever carrier we need to get to that destination. But, it's all on standby. So, if flight's full, you get bumped.

I got bumped going to Thailand once, and another time coming back from Manila. But, that's a small price to pay for the freedom to travel the world on a shoestring.

—How often can you bring family on flights?

Any time there are seats available. These days, not much. The planes fly pretty full any more, and you really have to plan ahead. If they get bumped and you're working the flight, you have to leave them behind.

—*This is something I'm really worrying about. Do most pilots go through divorces since they are barely home? I don't want the same thing to happen to me.*

Sadly, that "time away" is a big factor in divorces. Statistically, I have no idea, but I would guess that pilots have an "elevated" (scuze the pun) chance of divorce. But, it just means that you and your spouse have to be aware of that fact, and work that much harder on your relationship.

—*Are you a real airline captain?*

Yes. I upgraded on the A321 series of aircraft in early 2000, after having flown it for nearly a decade. I had also been a Captain for a year on the DHC-8 back in the early 90's when my company had them. My first "Captainship" was on a Twin Otter for the Virgin Islands Seaplane Shuttle in 1988 (see, *Stranded in Paradise*, this Volume).

My, but it seems my FO's are getting younger. I must be getting older.

—*What's your favorite part about a flight?*

Hmm...I'd have to say the landing, just because it's the most challenging time. Especially if we have to shoot an ILS to minimums. It's just a really satisfying feeling to be able to use your skills. I also really love to say "Hi" and "Buh-bye" to the passengers, especially the kids. I finally tracked down some plastic wings (sadly a thing of the past) to hand out to them.

—How do pilots stay up during long flights, and crossing multiple time zones?

It's a big challenge. Mainly you have to plan ahead and be well rested. Internationally, there are "IRO"s on flights—International Relief Officers, who fly the plane after takeoff. The Captain and FO go sleep in a bunk until landing time, then take back over from the IROs.

—What do you think about doing PA's? Do you like them?

Love to do PA's. Although, I wish I were a better "comedian." Some pilots just have "the touch" to crack passengers up. I learned a long time ago I get all tongue tied trying to be cutesie, so I stick with a (mostly) standard PA. Although I have to say I'm a fairly good "tour guide." I flew Grand Canyon tours for several years as one of my first commercial aviation gigs, and I had to entertain my passengers for three hours straight. (See, *Dealing with Passengers—Don't Panic!* in Volume II of this series.)

—Have you ever been told you won't ever be a pilot? How did you feel?

No, I was, blessedly, always encouraged and supported. In my 6 years of flight instructing, I always encouraged the student, however poorly they performed. I only told a student once that he was "not a very good pilot." I said this SPECIFICALLY because he was very cocky, and as a result very sloppy in his flying. It "scared him straight," however, so it did the trick, and he became a better pilot.

—Can a pilot change the plane he or she flies if they don't enjoy the routes, don't like the style or feel uncomfortable flying it?

Yes and no. Each job comes with its own opportunities and restrictions. At a major airline, you normally have several types of aircraft, several bases, etc. So, if you are senior enough to change planes, you are welcome to bid for it—if and when a bid comes out. Normally, once you change planes, you are restricted to that plane for several years, to cut down on training costs of pilots jumping around too much.

—When do you reference speed as a percent of Mach and when do you use knots?

(Note: Before I could answer this question on my Facebook page, we received an EXCELLENT reply to this by Peter F.—far better than I could have answered. So, here's Peter's reply.)

When pilots use knots, they usually mean indicated airspeed. Due to physics, the speed of sound, as reported in indicated, lowers with altitude, gradually approaching operational speeds of jet airliners. Some physical effects manifest when approaching the speed of sound, necessitating that pilots are aware of the speed ratio to sound speed.

Airplane will usually change from "knots" to "mach" by itself when the time is right (depends on speed and some other factors), and it happens usually in high twenties (measured in thousands of feet). This altitude is sometimes called crossover altitude.

Thanks, Peter!

—Thanks for all your stuff. Just wondering, how you manage your fitness while "on the road?"

So glad you're liking the blog. Fitness on the road is a challenge, but not insurmountable. Certainly there are times when you work all day and have minimal rest at the hotel, so you can't always get in the best workout. But, nearly all hotels now have some semblance of a gym—some so-so, some excellent. And, if the weather's nice, I'll often run outside for cardio.

I did P90X a couple years ago. You can do that and similar workout systems right in your room. It also changed my habits for the better. I now take a food bag with me, packed with healthy meals. Bonus: you save money on the road!

Another great round of questions came from Ken McQ., a TV aerial cameraman in KDTW, who was writing a college paper on CRM (Crew Resource Management):

—Are you familiar with the crash of Northwest Flight 255?

Yes. It was instrumental in forming the concept of "Sterile Cockpit" that is absolutely adhered to in the world's airlines today.

—Has CRM training changed or evolved much during your career?

Dramatically. I started this career when the general mindset was, "The Captain is God." Today, the Captain is an experienced pilot who is ultimately in charge, but also respectfully incorporates all his/her human resources–the FO, FA's, ATC, Company, etc., to safely operate the flight.

As I mentioned in Part 1 of this series, the perfect example of this evolution in thinking can be seen in the original *Star Trek's* Captain Kirk vs. *The Next Generation's* Captain Jean Luc Picard. (See also *Top 5 Improvements in Modern Safety*, this volume.)

—How are checklists performed in your cockpit? Are they paper or electronic?

For standard procedures, Paper. Checklists are read verbatim, and never "memorized," as it were. If we have, say, an engine failure, an electronic checklist will pop up on the ECAM. But we also have a QRH (Quick Reference Handbook) and other printed resources with which to follow up all "non-normals" and emergencies.

—Have the checklists changed much over time?

Again, dramatically.

My take on a funny meme that was making the rounds recently.

A lot of research on CRM, human error, and such have taken place in the last 30 years, and our checklists are direct result. They are simpler, more straight forward, and precise. We "Verify" the most important items

("Landing Gear–Verify, down, three green." "Verified–Down, three green.").

This, "Verify" system, I believe, comes directly from NASA studies.

—Is it always clear who's responsibility it is to complete the checklists?

Yes. The PM (Pilot Monitoring) always reads the checklists.

—Do you ever have to prompt the First Officer to complete a checklist?

Occasionally. Boredom, fatigue, distraction, and low morale can affect anybody at any time, and these are serious human factors that have to be overcome to get the job, however simple, safely done.

And, to wrap it up, a few fun questions

—Have you ever flown any celebrities?

I've flown many, but rarely known it until they left and the Flight Attendants told us. I've had a Tom Cruise here, a Britney Spears there. My favorite was former "Tonight Show" announcer Ed McMahon, who was a pilot in WWII and Korea. He marched right up to the cockpit and shook our hands. I told him, "You're twice the pilot I'll ever be!" (Note: Brigadier General McMahon passed away in 2009.)

My ultimate dream was to have Leslie Neilson stick his head in the cockpit and say his famous line from the movie *Airplane!*: "I just want to tell you both, good luck. We're all counting on you.". He was known for doing just that. (See, *Cap'n Aux's Ultimate Aviation Dream*, Volume II.)

That would have made my career!

—What was the funniest thing that happened to you during a flight?

Great Q. We're always pulling pranks on the new flight attendants. My favorite is to type "Large Rodent Loose in Cabin" into our MCDU computer scratch pad, and then bring her up to show her the message. Then we switch to the hydraulic page, which shows the word "RAT" (for Ram Air Turbine). Then we send her in back with a trash bag to catch the critter!

My April Fool's day joke backfired when, during the flight, I made PA's about our progress toward LAX . . . although we were going to Vegas! The FA's went nuts, calling us and demanding we correct ourselves. They finally begged us, as one little old lady was about to have a heart attack. It was then that I learned that, the voice on the PA is the voice of God!

—What was your most memorable flight?

I'll never forget the time I flew three orphaned bear cubs from Haines to Juneau, Alaska, in a Cessna 207. Their mom had been killed by a poacher, and so the Alaska Fish & Game had to ship them off to zoos. It was bitter sweet, as it was sad that they had been orphaned, but such a cool experience to fly these three cubs. They were sedated, in cages . . . and they stunk to high heaven! Sadly, the poacher was never caught. So, I just had to write a fictional account of this episode in my novel, The Last Bush Pilots, wherein the bush pilots exact poetic revenge on the poacher.

I SAVED MY FAVORITE QUESTION OF ALL FOR LAST . . . .

—Why are so many pilots mean but you're nice ?—Junior M.

JUNIOR, YOU JUST CHARMED YOURSELF INTO A FREE SIGNED COPY OF *"THE LAST BUSH PILOTS!"*

Junior reads the checklist while flying. IIe is well on his way to pursuing his career as an airline pilot!

Glad to hear I'm nice, but sorry others are so mean! I think the past 20, even 30, years have been brutal for airline pilots. Very volatile. Many have lost great jobs and are back at crappy ones, if they're flying at all. So, understandably, they're bitter. Also, the pay has come wayyy down—1/2 of what it was 30 years ago. So, I think the realities of this biz have fallen far short of expectations.

Conversely, I have to say that I have been extremely blessed in my career. As most pilots climbing up the ladder experience, my early years were very volatile. My paycheck looked like a yoyo for a good 10 years (up, down, non-existent, way up, way down). Also, I was blessed to get a relatively early start at a company that was the sole surviving post-deregulation upstart airline. I did spend a couple years on furlough in the early 90's, and this past decade has seen two mergers, which is *always* volatile to pilots (see *The Airline Pilot's Kryptonite*, this volume). Even so, I've loved the journey.

With a dozen years left as of this writing, I'm crossing my fingers.

Nope, this business ain't for the faint-hearted.

That is why I always stress in this blog, the airline career is like Forest Gump's proverbial box of chocolates: you never know what you're gonna get.

So . . .

ENJOY THE RIDE!

SECTION 6: #Crewlife
Or, lifestyles of the broke and overworked.

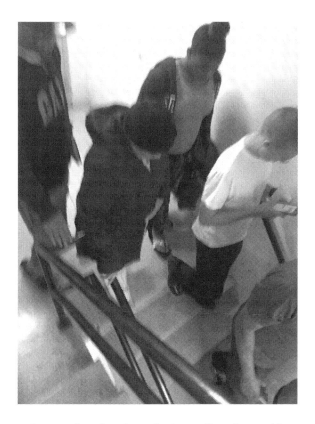

Evacuating our hotel at 1am during a fire alarm. After standing out in the rain for an hour, we were let back into our rooms (false alarm). Report time the next day: 9am.

There I Wuz! Stranded in Paradise

Originally published in Airways Magazine as "Pilots of the Caribbean", January, 2016

"So, there I was! Stranded, jobless, homeless, penniless, in the strange land called St. Thomas, U.S. Virgin Islands."

Cap'n Babyface on a "Flightseeing" tour over the Juneau Icefield, 1987.

As DC and Allen learn in my novel, *The Last Bush Pilots*, this dream flying career comes with a nightmarish "Catch-22," a maddening paradox: you can't *get* the flight experience without first *having* the experience. It plagues the upcoming pilot on every rung of the aviation ladder, from the first flight instructor job all the way to the lofty airline position. The pilot must beg, borrow and steal to build said flight time. And, that experience must also come with luck. But luck comes in two forms, good and bad, as we shall see in this next piece.

My *There I Wuz!* contribution to Volume 3.

Looking back on the long and winding road that brought me to the left seat of the Airbus, I have come to realize that a pilot's career is nothing but timing and luck.

But luck means taking chances. And that means risk. Rolling the dice.

My first lucky break came after six years of floundering at the bottom rung of the aviation ladder—single-engine CFI and local VFR charters. I decided to roll the dice. With a well-timed (i.e., lucky) phone call, I landed a job half a world away, in the notorious Alaska bush. Flying locals, frozen fish and frozen government workers out of Juneau, Alaska, in four short summer months I racked up over 500 hours of precious AK time. (See, *The Sky Fell*, Volume 1 of this series and in *Airways* Magazine, May 2014.)

Finally, "Termination Dust"—the snow line dropping ever lower along the peaks and signaling the end of flying season—encroached upon Juneau.

Time to find a new job.

With that magical word, "Alaska," now shining atop my résumé, job offers came in droves. But all were lateral moves; that is, flying single pilot, single engine VFR pistons. That was all well and good, but I hungered for that ultimate aeronautical pie in the sky: the airline flight deck. To claw my way to the next rung toward my aviation dream, I desperately needed twin engine time.

At the Pilot Bunkhouse with the 3 Amigos: Leon (L) & Pierre (w/Guitar)

Once again, I rolled the dice. Once again, I landed a job over the phone, half a world away, this time in the Caribbean. The Virgin Islands, to be exact.

Eyeing the Termination Dust and dropping thermometer, suddenly the tropical V.I.'s sounded, well, tropical. Even more enticing was the multiengine planes I would fly.

Twin time at last! Finally, the lucky break I was looking for.

But luck comes in many forms—good and bad.

Purchasing a $20 suit at Goodwill and tossing a bag packed with my entire worldly possessions across my back, I jumpseated south and east to a mythical land called St. Thomas, U.S. Virgin Islands.

The Juneau—Ketchikan—Seattle—Phoenix—Miami—St. Thomas jumpseat odyssey took three days. Exhausted, and drenched by muggy tropical heat, I took in my new home.

If you've lived all your life in the good old U.S. of A., your first taste of another country can be a bit of a shocker. And, while the V.I's are a U.S. territory, they're very much in their own world.

Even the remote villages of the AK bush could not prepare me for the scene I beheld. St. Thomas's Charlotte Amalie International Airport looked like the set of Casablanca, replete with indigent locals, gaudy uniformed officials and a "main terminal" comprised of a dilapidated quonset hut.

Leon checks me out in the Aztec.
Already traded that "Alaska tan" for a Caribbean one!

"Taxi? You want taxi?" an Island man shouted in my face in lilting Islandese. He would be the first of hundreds of such men crying the same phrase over the course of my year in paradise. When you're a whitey, I quickly found, you're a tourist.

My new boss—we'll call him Jack—easily found me, probably because I was the only young white boy wandering shell-shocked among the sweat-soaked locals. Aside from a movie pirate, Jack was the first man I'd ever seen who actually wore an earring.

Indeed, I had arrived in the Caribbean.

Perhaps the earring should have tipped me off, as the pirate analogy soon proved to be a bit too close to the mark. For, within two months, my little lucky piece of paradise would become, Paradise Lost.

Living in our company's pilot bunkhouse in Charlotte Amalie along with two other aviators, in two weeks I was checked out. I began racking up blessed twin time in Piper Aztecs, flying single pilot to such exotic locales as St. Barts, St. Maarten and San Juan. The stunning turquoise waters, verdant islands and fluffy-cloud skies of the Caribbean quickly became my new best friends as I island-hopped up and down the Lesser Antilles. Jimmy Buffett forever played between my ears, whether through a Sony Walkman or my own imagination.

But then I found evidence of a possible internal fuel leak in one of our planes.

Look closely: that ain't no Clark Y Airfoil, that's an exploded wing!

Jack implored me to ignore it; insisted his mechanic was on it. Then I found another. And another. Finally, while cranking up in San Juan, the engine backfired with a *pop!* Well, piston engines backfire all the time, but this one blew up my Aztec's right wing like a balloon. Yet another internal fuel leak.

Despite Pirate Jack's rantings and ravings, I quit on the spot. It was the only job I ever walked away from.

Of course, I was also ejected from the pilot bunkhouse.

So, There I was, stranded, jobless, homeless, in the strange land called St. Thomas, U.S. Virgin Islands.

Oh, you may think, stranded in paradise ain't so bad. But all that cash I had squirreled away in Alaska had quickly evaporated while waiting to be checked out, and awaiting my first meager paycheck. In the insanely 'spensive Caribbean, no less, where everything has to be imported. Even, inexplicably, the fruit.

My buddy Pierre, one of my fellow aviating roommates, quit with me. But, unlike me, he had an Ace in the hole: in a month's time, he had been invited to a ground school with the local kings of the air, the Virgin Islands Seaplane Shuttle (VISS). Pierre didn't have a seaplane rating, and neither did I. But the VISS was ramping up service in land-based, 19-passenger, twin-engine turboprop Twin Otters, and they were hiring a class of Captains and First Officers. With his time, Pierre would be walking into a twin engine turboprop Captain slot. Perhaps, Pierre suggested, I could tag along and snag a First Officer position.

A call to VISS Director of Ops John Stewart-Jervis* confirmed: all slots filled, but he invited me to show up, in case a First Officer position might open up. No promises.

Master of Salvage Pierre whips up a BBQ dinner, using a hubcap for the grill and a blowdryer for a bellows.

One month away. One month with no job, no shelter, no pay or promises, and the amber, Low-Level $$$ light flashing in my face.

I could easily jumpseat back home to Mommy. Lick my wounds, send out some résumés. Flight instruct.

Or, I could once again roll the dice.

Really, sleeping on a Caribbean beach for a month didn't sound all that bad, did it? Time for a well-earned, if shoestring, vacation.

I was in.

Immediately, Pierre and I caught a lucky break. Brenda, a local "Frenchie" (the Caribbean equivalent of a Creole) offered us her father's "cabin," an abandoned cement bunker in the middle of the St. Thomas wilderness. With no electricity, no water, and jungle and critters encroaching from every direction, it at least had a roof that, during daily thunderstorms, didn't leak. Mostly. Even better, the beach was a stroll away. That, and the local pub.

We moved in. Hacking the place into shape with machetes, we literally carved out our own piece of paradise.

Pierre was a master of salvage, having once driven a jalopy across the Sahara, where you must fix your broken transportation or die. Repairing his equally-dilapidated Island car with bailing wire and a wooden dowel, we at least had wheels with which to navigate the winding, left-driving island roads. And thus began our shoestring vacation.

One of the things we had going for us, we found, were cocoanuts. Lots and lots of cocoanuts, the top of which we would machete-hack. Free cocoa juice, and free meat inside. Tropical and tasty, if a tad too vegetarian for our tastes.

Of course, Happy Hour found the cheap local rum mixed inside as well.

----

*Cocoanut n Rum Happy Hour!
Followed by cocoanut hors d'oeuvres,
cocoanut filet sautéed in cocoanut, with
shredded cocoanut salad, and, for
dessert, chilled cocoanut (w/o the chill).
Where's Spam when you need it?*

The Master of Salvage and I were nothing, if not creative. Indeed, we had discovered the original cocoanut rum. As a result, I am not really able to relay the details of that fabled month in ersatz paradise, as they are a bit fuzzy, other than to say a good time was had by all.

Finally, well-rested and penniless, with cocoanut juice oozing from our pores, Pierre and I jumpseated 30 miles south, over to the island of St. Croix, where the VISS was based.

We walked into a ground school class set up for a crew of 24—twelve captains and twelve first officers.

To my chagrin, all the FO's showed up . . .

But only half of the captains.

Desperate, DO Jervis and Chief Pilot Marty searched the room for qualified captains.

Cap'n Babyface trades up!

A sly grin grew across my face, as I slid my logbook across the table like it was a winning poker hand.

I had more than twice the required total time, but only half the twin time. With a little extra training and paperwork, they decided, they'd make it work.

Instead of the hoped-for First Officer position, I had waltzed straight into the left seat of a turboprop airliner.

And *that* is how I landed my very first Capn's position, at the ripe old age of 26.

Yes, indeed, looking back, a pilot's career is nothing but timing and luck.

But, sometimes, you must create your own luck.

Every time I have rolled the dice, adventure ensues.

That, and success.

This piece is dedicated to the memory of VISS DO, Captain John Stuart-Jervis.

A former Royal Navy pilot, lost to us in 1995 while competing in Europe's most prestigious balloon race, tragically and inexplicably shot down by the Belarus military.

Interview with FO Woody
Originally published in Airways News

*"If I had any advice, just enjoy where you are.
Life is a good thing if you want to make it positive."*

Through my blog and writings, I like to convey the adventure that is inherent in flying. Moreover, I strive to inspire the up and coming pilots as they prepare for their own adventures. But, I always try to temper that inspiration with a healthy dose of reality. As we saw in the previous story, the airline career is nothing but timing and luck. This is a brutal, fickle business, and there are absolutely no guarantees that you'll "make it."

Woody's story is not only a cautionary tale of how your dream career can go south, it is also a sage lesson on how to deal with life's curveballs. As First Officer Woody conveys to us, you have to learn to let go of the control you don't have, and appreciate where you are at the moment.

Woody is a pilot for a major U.S. airline. He has made it to that lofty position that many an aviation enthusiast would consider the Holy Grail of aviation: the airline cockpit.

But dreams come with high price tags—not just financially, but emotionally.

"When I was a little kid, I wanted to be an astronaut," Woody said. "So, I had tons of airplane models, looked at anything that flew, and always wanted to go to the airport."

While his story begins like many a typical pilot, his climb up the aviation ladder has been, to say the least, strenuous. Three times, from three failed airlines, Woody has been furloughed (laid off). Three times, he's been forced to pick up his family, sell the house and move. And, while he's been flying for major U.S. carriers for 16 years now, at his current airline, he still languishes in the bottom 15% of the seniority list.

Yes, Woody has had it tough. While many would say he has "made it," made it to what? He's still not in the left seat—the Captain's chair—and has yet to receive a line, or a schedule. For the dozen + years he's been at his current airline, he's been stuck on reserve; that is, waiting for the phone to ring to replace a pilot who called in sick. In other words: the bottom of the bottom.

Was it worth it?

"It was an unbelievable set of circumstances that got me to my airline," Woody says. "I worked hard to get here, and I feel blessed to be here. But, even so, I've been junior my whole career."

At 48 years old, with a wife, Kirstin, and two teenagers, Ian and Sophie, to support, it hasn't been easy. Worse, life itself has thrown the family some very tough curve balls.

"We got married in '93," Woody reflected. "In '99, our first daughter, Gillian, was born. Within a year, at St. Louis Children's Hospital, she passed away."

When that happened, he said, they had a choice.

"We could be a team and get through it," he says," or we could not be a team, and life could be completely chaotic and spiral out of control. I know a lot of people that, when hard times come, they start to drink. They become dependent on something they think is going to make them feel better."

Whenever something bad happens, he says, he and Kirstin try to ground themselves in reality.

"Anything that took us out of reality just wasn't a good thing," he says. "So, for some reason, we've always been a good team."

After the loss of their daughter, Woody and Kirstin became advocates for others searching for answers to their own children's medical issues. To their surprise, Woody says, the very act of helping others turned out to be some of the most healing therapy they've ever encountered.

Still, the couple was in for hard times. Within a few scant years of losing Gillian, Woody was furloughed, hired by another airline, and furloughed again. All told, three furloughs in as many years. For a pilot bent on an airline career, the volatility was stressful, to say the least. Worse, each new job placed him back on the bottom.

Woody says, "Everything's based on seniority, so you want to get to your airline as soon as you can. So, you have to be a go-getter. Go from a flight instructor to a commuter job to an airline job. But life for me hasn't been a straight, linear line. It's been a lot of curves and lots of ups and downs. Two steps back one step forward."

Through the ordeal, Woody says, he's learned to appreciate what he has, right where he has it. Moreover, he's learned to live his life in the moment, savoring the blessings he and his family do have.

Woody's son is in a similar position, he says. "Ian wants to be an Engineer. And, as an A student in advanced classes, Ian believes his future is all mapped out."

Woody and his beautiful family.

Pilots tend to think the same way, Woody says. Striving for a goal is good, but Woody is concerned that Ian may one day look back on his life and wonder where it went.

"You're trying to teach your kids to do the right thing, but there has to be a balance," Woody advises. "Work toward your goals, of course. I'm not saying be a slacker, but we're pushing these kids these days to be overachievers."

As a former University of Colorado alpine racing athlete, Woody knows about focusing on a life goal. But he compares it to the Japanese way of life. "Push, push, push, and suddenly you have a lot of suicides and people are unhappy, and what's it all for?"

His advice: Stop and smell the roses.

"If you're going to put those blinders on to reach that goal, then you're not going to look around. You're going to miss relationships, miss some beautiful people in your life that are going to pass you by, because you were so obsessed with getting to a goal."

So, Woody has made peace with where is at the moment. But, with all the turmoil and extra effort it's taken for him to land that airline job—only to get stalled at the bottom of the top—does he still actually like his job?

"It goes back and forth," he admits. "For awhile, I didn't really like coming to work."

However, Woody feels like he's turned a corner. With each flight, he's learning to come out of his shell.

Woody's "Office View." All in all, not too shabby!

"Getting out on the road, having a mini-adventure with the crew, getting to know them and not closing them out like I used to. I've found that has helped."

Despite the camaraderie and financial benefit of flying regularly, however, Woody actually prefers his reserve schedule, he says, as opposed to a flying regular line. Being on call often allows him much more time at home with his family.

"It's less money, but it pays the bills just fine. I'm not going to kill myself to make ten more hours a month, only to be gone 75% more time."

And what about the job itself?

"When you close the door and get flying," he says, "it's a great job!"

Woody realizes that, despite the volatility wrought on the airline industry through 9/11 and the economic crisis of '08, he actually has it better than others.

"We as pilots always think we've been hit really hard," he says. "Yeah, we have, but everybody's been hit hard. Nobody has it easy. And those guys in the business world often hate their jobs. I can't say that about mine."

But pilots also tend to make it harder than it has to be, he says. While he likes his job, he says, he doesn't live for it. And therein lays the trick.

"I think it could be better, but if you think that way and it makes you angry, you just have to kind of let that go. Pilots are our own worst enemy. (Referring to the self-defeating infighting among pilot groups during a recent merger—see, *The Airline Pilot's Kryptonite*, this volume.) I think our jobs could be ten times better. It didn't have to be this hard, and it could have been much better for everybody."

And what does he expect for his future?

"Long term, I would like to make Captain, that's a given," he says. "The ego of it all, I don't care. But, for financial and retirement reasons, that would be a wise thing to do."

Woody says he's not been able to provide for Kirstin and the kids the way he'd like, but he has been able to pay the bills and put a roof over their heads.

"But I don't want us to have to worry about money," he says.

Even so, he plans to hold off on any Captain upgrades till Sophie graduates from high school.

"At that point," Woody says, "it would be all about retirement. Then again, something might happen in the next few years that changes that formula. But, that's the frustrating thing about being pilots; we're the last to know."

Like many aviators, Woody would like to own his own airplane.

"I've always wanted to get my kids into aviation," he says. "Or at least expose them to it on a different level than just going to an airport and walking onto an airliner. Using that small airplane as a tool to have fun and travel. There's a ton of places to go within a few hours' flight in a small plane."

At his old job, he says, many fellow pilots used to fly their family to weekend fly-ins. For him, that communal spirit was its greatest draw.

But for now, that dream will have to continue flying its perpetual holding pattern. A graduate of the School of Extra-Hard Knocks, Woody says he's flown with plenty of pilots who've had it relatively easy—and are up to their eyeballs in debt.

"Yeah, some bad things happened to us," he allows," but we went from being clueless to being pretty fiscally responsible. We drive old cars, we live very frugally. But, I'm not judging anyone. If I'd had it easy, I can almost guarantee you I'd be a different person. I'd probably have spent oodles of money and been really irresponsible, and probably had a big head on my shoulders."

Woody says their challenges have served to keep him grounded, and humble.

"I see pilots that don't seem to think that anything could ever happen to their careers or lives," he says," and when it does, they're surprised."

Conversely, Woody admits to being challenged to look toward an optimistic future, rather than always waiting for the other shoe to drop.

"The long term implications of Gillian's death, and the three furloughs, the moves . . . they're still manifesting themselves," he says. "A little bit of self-doubt, of letting myself go. I'm still afraid to commit to new friendships. That was never my character trait before."

Despite his own challenges, he has some excellent advice for the upcoming generation of pilots.

"If I had any advice, just enjoy where you are. Don't focus on the bad things. There's nothing you can do about it, you've got to move on. Life is a good thing if you want to make it positive."

Alongside a healthy attitude comes personal health as well, he says.

"Keep eating well!" he exclaims. "Don't get soft. Always remember your roots, and try not to step on people."

The self-induced karma, he says, will pay off in the end.

As for flying, Woody had one last thing to say.

"Being a pilot's an interesting thing," he says. "You walk into the cockpit, meet somebody and think, 'Man, this guy's gonna be hard to fly with.' And maybe they are, for a lot of people. But a lot of those guys turn out to be some of the best friends and pilots that I've known. They were just going through shitty times."

Woody implores us to remember that we're not the only one going through hard times.

"Everybody's going through something. That's one thing I've learned. Instead of feeling sorry for yourself, just remember that there's very few people that have it perfect."

While Woody and his family may have had it tougher than most, in many ways their lives are a study of life itself. Through their challenges and ordeals, they've learned, grown. Grown wiser, and grown closer.

Pilots—or anyone pursuing a career—could learn a few things from Woody's story.

As you strive toward that dream, don't forget that you're already living it.

My Favorite Destination

I know I don't get there often enough
But God knows I surely try
It's a magic kind of medicine
That no doctor could prescribe

But there's this one particular harbor
So far but yet so near
Where I see the days as they fade away
And finally disappear

"One Particular Harbor"—Jimmy Buffet

There's been a vision in my head all my adult life. A very vivid dream, I think. But it may very well be a real memory. A vague picture of a secret destination that I stumbled upon while flight training in a small college nearby.

To this day, I haven't figured it out.

Nestled in the rugged Chiricahua mountains in southeastern Arizona is a tiny dirt strip that only the most intrepid, determined pilots can find, let alone slip into.

You must take the base-to-final turn on faith that something's actually there. It takes all of your skills to safely land. But once you do, the camaraderie you find there is magical. You are part of a family.

There's picnic tables, fireplaces, a beautiful mountain stream, all covered by a lush canopy of Ponderosa pines. Indeed, the strip itself is surrounded by pines, all the more tough to spot and land.

You roll to a stop, kill the engine, hop out. The warm sun greets you from a cloudless blue sky. Children laugh and play. Barbecue wafts on the dusty breeze. Somewhere, somebody plays a guitar. And of course, the sound of prop planes buzzing in and out fill the air like dozens of magical fairies.

It's the warmest, coziest, most peaceful feeling my mind can conjure.

And perhaps conjure it has. As I said, I can't be sure if it's a dream or an actual memory. It may even be mixed with my most cherished childhood memories, of backpacking with my family deep in the wilds of the Ansel Adams Wilderness, south of Yosemite.

In my travels, I've racked up many particular harbors: Juneau, Alaska; St. Croix, USVI; Interlaaken, Switzerland; Telluride Colorado; and St. Barts, Antilles (rumored to be Jimmy Buffett's famed "Cheeseburger in Paradise.")

And perhaps my favorite, a sleepy little coastal fishing village tucked way back in the wilds of Venezuela, with no paved roads, no phones, and not a soul who speaks English.

My pilot buddies and I jumpseated there for a weekend.

We stayed for a week.

Da boyz (l-r Aux, Brian, Kevin, Randy), try on some irie Venezuelan seaweed dreadlocks.

We hitchhiked 30 miles to the next town to call in sick. Crew scheduler Paula, (Chris's wife, God rest her soul), covered our a$$es, all for the bargain basement price of a bottle of Venezuelan rum.

Today, decades later, if I detect a slight dust in the air, I'm instantly transported back.

Back to that magical land, that One, True, Particular Harbor.

And I am.

Completely.

At peace.

In some ways, it doesn't matter whether my destination is real or imagined. Because it exists in my head, it's real. As real as the oatmeal I had for breakfast.

And the world is a better place, knowing it exists.

Have you found your particular harbor? If not . . . find it! It's out there. Out there waiting for you to discover.

And never forget:

The world is a Disneyland made just for YOU!

This piece is dedicated to the memory of Paula Hamilton.

Flying Ain't What it Used to be. Or is it?

Originally published on AirwaysMag.com

I am a pilot in love with a feisty French woman named, Fifi. She is fickle, and many other lovestruck pilots clamor for her attention.Somehow, despite our ups and downs, we have stayed together for over 20 years.

Fifi is the Airbus A321 family of aircraft.

Her critics facetiously call her a "flying computer." Many readers of my capnaux.com blog believe that, with her sophisticated fly-by-wire system, Fifi flies herself, and I am just a passenger.

I disagree.

Today's modern aircraft are becoming increasingly automated and sophisticated, I'll give you that. At this level of flying, the Captain and crew are indeed more Flight Managers than Pilots. That is to say, except for takeoff and landing, the autopilot is on 99% of the time. (Some aircraft, including Fifi, can also autoland.)

Use of the autopilot frees up the crew from focusing on the mundane task of keeping her upright, in order to concentrate on more pressing issues: watching for traffic, monitoring systems, navigating, working the radios, etc. In short, staying on top of the Big Picture.

Moreover, we have highly sophisticated and reliable navigation systems such as GPS (Global Positioning Satellites) and IRS (Inertial Reference Systems), that whisk us from Point A to Point B with extreme accuracy.

So, is this truly flying?

Some would say that, with all the computers and button pushing, the romance and adventure has been sucked out of flying.

Some would be right. And, some would be wrong. Life itself is an adventure, and life in the sky, exponentially so—regardless of your metal.

However, as an industry, we have been inexorably moving toward a future dominated more by automation and less by fundamental flying skills. And, with the advent of drones and the 2015's Germanwings 9525 tragedy, however, some people are even clamoring for pilotless cockpits. I believe that pie in the sky is, at least for civilian airliners, still a century away (think, "Welcome aboard our fully automated airline. Nothing can go wrong *click!* go wrong *click!* go wrong.") Even so, amazing advances in technology have brought our accident rates down to an all-time low.

We have recently found, however, that this high tech environment is its own double-edged sword. As pilots depend more and more on their automated machines, their basic stick and rudder skills have degraded. Moreover, as we have recently learned from our dramatic video interview series with Qantas Airlines Captain Richard de Crespigny—whose A380 suffered an engine explosion that damaged all but one system—today's airline pilot must not only keep those basic skills honed, but must also strive to understand their increasingly complex aircraft.

In our interview, Captain de Crespigny said,"If you want to go to a high tech aircraft that is run by computers, there is a responsibility to understand the underlying systems. Because, when those systems fail—and they do fail —it's up to the pilot now to recover an aircraft that is very complex and much more sophisticated. So these new, very complicated aircraft need highly skilled people who can get to the core, understand the core, and that means when these computers fail, they can reverse-engineer these machines and treat it just like a flying lawn mower, and work out how to get the machine down onto the ground." (See, *Black Swan Event: The Captain De Crespigny Story*, this volume.)

Many pilots pine for the "good old days" when we all drove "flying lawn mowers." When ATC didn't have an iron grip on our flight path, where we could fly autonomously—without so much as a radio—anywhere we chose, and when the FAA didn't tie down our precious birds with bureaucratic red tape. Even so, that Nostalgic Nirvana still exists in pockets around the world, from the Alaska bush to the Australian Outback.

Looking back on my career, I feel especially blessed to have lived in a historical sweet spot—somewhere between *too dangerous* and *too boring*— where survival by one's seat-of-the-pants and stick-and-rudder skills were more important than programming a flight computer, where *flying* the plane trumped *managing* the plane.

However, just as the characters in my novel, *The Last Bush Pilots*, we seem to be nearing the end of an era of freedom and adventure in the sky.

We are becoming the bear cubs orphaned and caged by the inexorable march of bureaucratic red tape we call Progress.

Hudson River visual to KLGA. Jumpseater Mac got some great snaps!

Recently, I've taken my first timid dip back into GA (General Aviation). Flying my good buddy Cap'n David's gorgeous Cessna 310, it's been like getting back in touch with one's roots, coming full circle back to that first family of lawn mowers that launched me into the sky. To my surprise, I've found it to be an almost daunting challenge. Multitasking is critical in any cockpit, and in a plane that lacks auto trim and auto thrust (basically anything not Airbus), the multitasking increases. Throw in the managing of cowl flaps, manifold pressure, props and fuel into the mix, as well as going back to the instrument pilot's "basic scan"of six flight instruments, and this spoiled, highfalutin Fifi Cap'n is suddenly quite humbled.

Lawn mower, perhaps. But a damned sophisticated one at that.

That is not to say David's Cessna doesn't have its own impressive level of high-tech. I have been especially impressed with the center stack of Garmin Communication and Navigation radio gear that, in many ways, are even more advanced than Fifi herself. Add to that Cap'n David's integration of his iPad's ForeFlight app, which sports a GPS moving map and real-time integrated weather displays. To do that on Fifi, we'd have to tap into the onboard wifi with our Company iPad and visit a site such as flightaware.com.

But FAA red tape has banned us from doing just that.

What I've found in 30-plus years of flying is that—whether talking GA or airliners—stick and rudder skills and basic knowledge of aircraft systems are critical to today's, and yesterday's pilots.

Regardless of size or sophistication, the pilot or pilots must always Aviate, Navigate, and Communicate. In short, *fly the plane.*

And therein lies the adventure.

The morning moon, highlighted by a contrail.

Whether you're talking gliders, Cessnas, Boeings or Airbuses, a pilot is a pilot, and the goal of getting to Point B is by no means guaranteed. Weather, mechanical failure, and any number of issues can be thrown at the Captain, who must use his or her ingenuity, experience and CRM (Crew Resource Management) to get out of said pickle.

And, as seasoned Chief Pilot Dusty Tucker says to cheechacko (greenhorn) bush pilot DC in *The Last Bush Pilots*, "The adventure's still out there, son. You just gotta go find it."

Just this week, my First Officer and I found it in the form of the amazing conjunction of Venus and Jupiter from FL 390 (39,000'), where the thin atmosphere and black sky afforded a spectacular front row seat.

I submit to you that, no matter how much red tape and automation can be thrown at your airplane, life in the sky is *by nature* an adventure—whether you're talking Cessna or Airbus.

Stay adventurous, my friends!

SECTION 7: Novel Idea! Book Excerpts

The Last Bush Pilots
Winner—Amazon Top 100 Breakthrough Novels 2013!

Two young pilots. One bold dream.
But if Alaska doesn't beat them, their friendship may.

"Suspense and drama in spades. Romantic entanglements and a covert mission help this aviation tale take off."—Kirkus Reviews

I wrote *The Last Bush Pilots* out of sheer awe.

Awe of a world as magnificent and alien to me as Planet Pandora.

The world: Alaska.

The Alaskan people—especially the pilots—were larger than life, and seemed to thrive in the harsh and indescribably lovely land with which each had fallen in love.

Indeed, I did, too.

I simply *had* to share with the world the magnificence that was Alaska.

Ralph Olafsen is one of the representative pilot characters in the novel. Quirky, colorful, full of contradictions . . . and fiercely independent.

Like many of the fascinating characters I encountered in Alaska, Ralph scorns authority, especially when it

is from government bureaucrats who think they know better than those who've learned Mother Nature's true Laws of the Skies the hard way. This antagonism can grate, and, in *The Last Bush Pilots*, gets our quirky hero—and his intrepid flying outfit SEAS—into big *doo-doo* with the authorities.

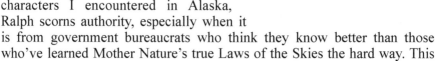
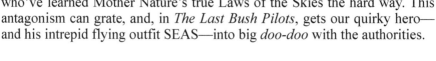

Excerpt—Chapter 7: Ralph Olafsen

Ralph Olafsen was a walking contradiction.

He was a hermit. And a joker. He was a soldier. And a peacenick. He was a creative artist who wasted his talent sketching unflattering characatures of those he thought little of, or those he admired. People rarely knew into which category they fell.

A wallflower if given the chance, Ralph kept to himself. Any patron stepping into the Red Dog Saloon on Drunk Pilot Night would invariably spot the legendary Jake Whitakker first. And Ralph last. Even his faded, chocolate brown flight jacket, so often the proud trademark of the bush pilot, instead seemed to camouflage him in the dark tavern or the airport lounge. But if a pilot's skills were truly based on the distress of his leather, Ralph's tattered rag would proclaim him a sky god.

Ralph's flying career, however, had started quite by accident; he was drafted. If not for Viet Nam, he would have been happy making trinkets in Arkansas with his wife Misty. But the backwoods hillbilly with the A.S. degree in Arts took to Army helicopters like a salmon to stream.

Much to Misty's relief, Ralph missed a tour of 'Nam by three short months. Instead, the Army sent him to Anchorage for a liaison tour of Elmendorf Air Force Base. There, he quickly won friends with weekly wilderness "recons" in his Sea King pontoon helicopter, fishing tackle and poles included. All on the taxpayer dime.

After his tour, despite the glut of ex-'Nam chopper pilots saturating the market, Ralph lucked into a distant cousin's logging operation in Arkansas. He quickly racked up time hauling machinery in and out of the hills in an old Sikorsky. A floatplane was added to the fleet, and Ralph took to it as naturally as his first whirlybird.

A corporation from Little Rock eventually bought out the mine. Treating him like a backwoods hick, the company's Chief Pilot tacked Ralph onto the bottom of the seniority list; he would only get to fly the worst of jobs. After eyeing the man for a moment, he tossed his company badge on the desk.

"To hell with it," he said, and marched out the door.

The counterculture couple packed up their van and headed for Alaska. The Last Frontier proved the perfect land to hone his skills as a pilot . . . and as a practical joker. And one incident in particular solidified his reputation for both.

It came to be called, The Great Mount Edgecombe Volcanic Eruption of April First.

Sitka Sheriff John McCabe valued his beauty sleep. But every summer morning, he was rudely shaken out of bed by the drone of Ralph's single engine Beaver, or the whop-whop of his whirlybird. In hot retaliation, McCabe accused Olafsen of everything from reckless flying to poaching. Though perhaps somewhat guilty of the former, Ralph was completely innocent of the latter, and the accusation incensed him.

In the early dawn twilight of April first, the very first day of the summer season, Sheriff McCabe was once again rudely shaken out of bed. But this time by a phone call. The harried voice of the desk sergeant snapped him to.

"Mount Edgecumbe's on fire, John," he cried. "The whole thing's erupting!"

"Impossible," McCabe replied with unmasked anger. "It's extinct."

"Take a look for yourself, then," the man answered.

He did. Shuffling out the front door in his emerald green pajamas and Martha's pink slippers, he looked west across Sitka Sound. And gasped in horror.

Mount Edgecombe, long dormant and dominating the skyline west of the city, highlighted in predawn twilight, belched an enormous cloud of black smoke.

"Jesus," he exclaimed, grabbing his keys and racing to his patrol car. He screeched away. "Prepare for an evacuation," he cried over the radio as he careened down Katlian Street. "Call the National Guard. And phone Ralph Olafsen. Tell him to get his chopper ready. We've got to see if this thing's gonna blow."

Over O'Connel Bridge and onto Japonski Island he raced, circling the airport perimeter and finally skidding up to the helipad.

Ralph was already strapped in the cockpit, sipping from his coffee mug, chopper blades spinning lazily. McCabe hopped in.

"Nice uniform, Chief," Ralph said.

"Shut up and move," he growled.

Ralph pulled the collective, the blades cut the air and the ship launched toward the rumbling menace. As they edged closer to the mouth of the volcano, McCabe fidgeted nervously in his seat. But Olafsen remained strangely calm.

He said over the intercom, "Relax, Chief. If this thing goes, we won't know what hit us. Well, except for the writhing in hellfire part as we plummet to our death."

McCabe shot him a scowl. "Move closer."

They did, enough to see over the rim. McCabe's eyes widened in surprise. His mouth dropped open.

"Well, looky there," Ralph said, "looks like someone decided to dump their old tires and burn 'em up. Nice they did it away from town, so's no one gets upset."

McCabe's eyes narrowed; the veins in his neck bulged against his pajama collar. Just as it looked like his head would explode, he shouted, "Take us back home!"

They landed at the helipad amidst a media melee. McCabe stared out the window in horror, realizing what was to come.

"Well, Chief, let's see. Half hour's flight time will be $125.00, special government rate. Shall I bill you, or the Department?"

"I owe you nothin'," McCabe spat, hopping out.

"Happy April Fool's Day, Chief," Ralph called as the Sheriff was mobbed by snickering reporters.

Cameras snapped away, and a half dozen microphones were thrust into McCabe's face, but all he could say was a clipped, "False alarm, no comment," before escaping.

The next day, the Sitka Daily Sentinel proudly sported a front page full color shot of McCabe in his "new uniform" of green and pink, the "volcano's" black smoke belching in the background.

Sheriff Erupts Over Volcanic Hoax, read the caption.

Every government agency, from the FAA to the EPA, investigated. But, aside from a two-hour discrepancy in the helicopter's flight log and two witnesses who heard a distant "whop-whop sound" on or about three a.m., no evidence was found.

Knowing when he was beat, and preferring to keep further shots of his "new uniform" out of the paper, Sheriff McCabe quickly and quietly squelched his own department's investigation. No charges were pressed.

Olafsen never once admitted guilt, but for months afterward he drank free in every bar in southeast Alaska.

CODE NAME: DODGER
A Young Adult "Spy/Fly" Adventure Series

TEENER-SKATER-PUNKER - SPY

My name's Justin Reed, a fourteen-year-old New York street kid, orphaned when my dad was murdered by the evil spy Pharaoh.

CIA Case Officer Bob Cheney discovered the Pharaoh was after me, too, so he took me into protective custody.

The Artful Dodger was my code name, and Bob, code name Fagin, trained me in all sorts of cool spy stuff: advanced self-defense, weapons, surveillance, evasion and survival. "The Company" even taught me how to use some sneaky spy gadgets.

But I had other plans.

Using my old street smarts—and new CIA training—I escaped CIA custody to cut out on my own.

But fate had "other plans" for me as well.

> *"Smooth and almost flawless execution of the plot line, with a multi-dimensional protagonist that sets this book apart from the rest. Fast paced, well choreographed action and bits of simple humor."*
> —Online Book Club

> *"I'm 50 years older than the target market for this book, and I couldn't put it down!"*
> —George Nolly, airline pilot-author, *Hamfist* trilogy

Mission 2: Cartel Kidnapping

CIA Agent Bob Cheney is kidnapped, and teen orphan Justin Reed—aka the Artful Dodger—tracks his newly-adoped father to a top secret smuggling base, where he is forced to match wits with the cartel family's brilliant teen prodigy, Luis Ocho. But Luis's stunning sister Kiara is another story. Is she falling for Justin, or is this just another one of Luis's diabolical tricks to lure the Artful Dodger to his demise?

"4 OUT OF 4 STARS! Fast-paced, action-packed spy novel. Grabs the reader hook, line, and sinker. Reluctant and avid readers who enjoy teenage fast-paced, spy adventure will love reading this book."
—Online Book Club

"Like Harry Potter, this YA series is fun for kids of all ages!"
—Tawni Waters, author, *Beauty of the Broken*

Mission 3: Jihadi Hijacking

Justin has settled into the quiet suburban life as secret agent Bob Cheney's newly-adopted son. Finally, he's put the nightmare of the spy world behind him for good. Or has he?

When their airliner is hijacked by armed terrorists—including a mysterious teen girl with striking green eyes—it's up to Justin and Bob to take it back. But that's only half the problem: once they overcome the terrorists, who's left to fly the plane?

Yet again, Justin must rely on his old orphan street smarts—and new CIA training—to take on armed terrorists and prevent apocalypse.
Every passenger's nightmare—and every simulator pilot's fantasy!

"4 OUT OF 4 STARS! Superb on so many levels. A a well-executed juggling act with just the right amount of humor. A highly detailed, entertaining, and character-driven spy thriller!"
—Online Book Club

"A free-wheeling, engaging espionage tale that aims to enlighten readers!"
—Kirkus Review

Mission 4: YAKUZA DYNASTY—EXCERPT

The Artful Dodger faces his greatest foe yet: Himself!

AGENCE INTERNATIONALE DE L'ANTI-TERRORISME

TOP SECRET—EXTREMELY URGENT

TO: KING COLE/ITA HQ
FM: AGENT TORA
LOC: KYOTO, JAPAN
RE: OPERATION DIVINE WIND
JAPAN'S NEW YAKUZA MAFIA SHOGUN, CODE NAME SAKURA, HAS ORDERED A WORLDWIDE HIT CONTRACT ON AGENT ARTFUL DODGER, REASONS UNKNOWN.
END MSG.

Troubled by confusing childhood memories, Justin and and his adopted secret agent father Bob search for clues to his past.

But his past, they discover too late, is searching for him.

Lost in the mean streets of Kyoto and inexplicably pursued by Korean and Japanese mobsters, Justin must use every ounce of his training and street skills to battle mafia thugs, modern-day ninjas—and a striking, pink-haired Japanese teen adventuress named Michiko.

Fighting for his very life, Justin unearths a secret from his childhood so shocking that not even his CIA training could prepare him.

PROLOGUE: THE STREETS OF KYOTO

It had been almost nine years since I'd set foot in my home country, and my Japanese was mighty rusty. So, practicing the old CIA skills, I did my best to eavesdrop on the passers-by, and to get back up to speed on the language.

We'd also moved away after mom died, and before I'd learned very much *Kanji*, the complicated characters they'd "borrowed" from the Chinese to write with. It still blew my mind that both the Chinese and Japanese could read each other's newspapers without knowing a lick of the other's language. To my relief, here in the big city of Kyoto, they had started printing most of the street names in English.

Eying the signs at the corner, I turned left to head toward Kyoto station.

The hair on my neck raised. I glanced behind, wondering if someone was following me. Nothing but Japanese businesspeople, scurrying every which way. But something had triggered my radar. After Pharaoh's henchmen had tried to kill me, I'd learned to trust my life with the instinct.

I ducked down a side alley. Now, if there was anyone actually tailing me, I could spot them in a second.

Hopping on my skate, I pushed off down the alley.

I kept glancing behind. Nothing.

"Shake it off, Dodger," I whispered to myself. "There's no Pharaohs, drug smugglers or terrorists after you."

Up ahead, a girl screamed.

"Help!" she cried in Japanese. "They've got me!"

Shoving off hard, I raced on my board toward the commotion. Halfway up the alley, I skidded to a stop. Between buildings on the left stood three teen thugs. Their backs to me, they slowly advanced on someone. All I could see over their shoulders was a flash of pink hair.

"Go away!" she cried. "I—I'll call the cops!"

The boys laughed.

"Not till after we're done playing with you, princess," one said.

I did a quick mental frisk. Nothing beneath their ratty T-shirts but a jungle of tattoos writhing around each kid's arms. But, judging by the bumps in the back pocket of their tight jeans, three switchblades.

I heard a *smack*. Their victim screamed in pain.

I kicked my board up into my hands.

"Let her go, *now!*" I shouted in Japanese, using my best cop voice.

"*Aré?* (huh?)" one of them asked in confusion.

The three punks turned.

I brandished my skate like it was a broadsword.

"Let her go, *now!*" I repeated.

The three laughed.

One whispered, "Hear that American accent? He's a *gaijin*. A foreigner."

The biggest one, the leader I guess, yelled, "Or what, *Ainoko?*" calling me a half-breed. "You'll skate us to death?"

"This doesn't concern you," another replied.

The third chimed in. "Go away and find your mommy, before we shove that board up your *shiri*."

With a shriek, the girl they had cornered broke through their line and raced toward me.

Her wild outfit threw me for a loop. She wore a frilly, red and black overall skirt and a ratty black leather jacket. Mismatched stockings ran above pink clod-stomper boots that glowed nearly as brightly as her pink-colored, bobbed hair.

Harajuku Punk, they called the crazy, cutesy-tough style. A bizarre mishmash of clothes and cultures, the looks were always changing, but the dress always wild.

I could tell that, even with a look of terror on her face, she was still one stunning Japanese beauty.

Continuing her panicked screaming, she raced past me, around the corner and down the alley.

She never even said, "*Arigato.*"

"Look what you've done," the leader said.

The second one added, "Now we gotta go find a new play toy."

The third added, "But first, you pay, *ainoko.*"

Flipping out their switchblades, they charged me, single file.

Holding my board like a baseball bat, I ducked below the first one's thrust and swatted his knees. With a shriek, he fell to the ground, blade sailing away. I stepped aside, and the second stumbled over his buddy. As he fell, I beaned the back of his noggin with my skate for good measure. Two down.

With a *Kamikaze* war cry, the third lunged at me, chopping down from above. Grabbing both sets of wheels with my hands, I blocked the blade, his knife penetrating through the laminated center and almost slicing my nose. He tried to yank it loose, but the blade was stuck.

I kicked straight up his crotch line. On his way to the pavement, I *bop-bopped* him with both ends of the board.

Eyeing the damage, I stepped around the groaning, writhing, whining punks to continue my journey.

"This was my brand new Powell," I growled, yanking the knife from the board and tossing it in a dumpster as I sauntered away. "You douchewipes know how much these things cost?"

I kicked into a jog, wondering if I should risk trying to ride on my precious, wounded board.

Rounding the corner back into the alley, I ran smack into the crazy-dressed *Harajuku* girl.

I nearly bowled her over, but caught myself. I stepped back, bowed and said, "*Sumimasen.*"

As I straightened, she raised a hand.

In it, she held a pistol.

A tiny, 9 mm Ruger LC9. Painted bright pink, of course.

She aimed it at my gut. With a dimpled smile that could sell toothpaste, she said, "Apology accepted, *gaijin.*"

Sighing, I dropped the board and raised my hands.

She said, "My name's Michiko. But my friends call me Mickey. *Hajimemashite,*" she finished, nodding her head.

"Nice to meet you, too, Mickey-san," I mumbled with a sigh, nodding slightly in a mock bow.

Holding a free hand to cover her mouth, Mickey giggled. Every finger was adorned with random metal rings, from butterflies to skulls. "Sakura was right. All you have to do is scream like a damsel in distress, and Justin Malcomb Reed will come running straight into your arms."

My eyes went wide. "What? How did you know my—"

A black Mercedes skidded around the corner and screeched up next to us.

I glanced around for an escape, but the three punks hobbled up to surround me, a look of murder in their eyes.

Gently holding a hand to my cheek, Mickey giggled again. "I quite enjoyed our brief encounter, Justin Reed-san. You are *much* cuter in person."

The door to the Mercedes opened. Mickey stepped back. With the pink Ruger, she motioned for me to get in.

From inside the car, a ghost from my past said, "Welcome home, Chika."

My jaw dropped. My legs grew weak. I collapsed to my knees in shock.

"*Mom*," I whispered.

Now Available!

Books Link: amazon.com/author/ericauxier

AFTERWORD

Alas, we have come to the end of our adventure . . . for now.

I hope you've enjoyed Volume III. If you purchased this in print on Amazon, you can pick up the eBook version for just $1.99 through their Match program. The eBook includes color photos and bonus materials, such as extra stories, hotlinks and videos. And, if you haven't read them yet, Volumes I and II are available there as well!

I'll be back next year with Volume IV. In the mean time, join me at capnaux.com, and watch for my articles in Airways Magazine, and online at AirwaysMag.com.

Drop me a line any time at eric@capnaux.com.

More links to my stuff such as Twitter, Facebook, Instagram, vimeo, etc. are listed on the next page.

This is Cap'n Aux . . . . signing off!

LINKS to All Things Cap'n Aux

BLOG

capnaux.com

BOOKS

amazon.com/

author/ericauxier

CONTACT

eric@capnaux.com

SWAG

cafepress.com/

CapnAuxswag

100% of author "swag" proceeds goes to orphan charities!

Facebook

facebook.com/

CapnAux

Twitter

twitter.com/

capnaux

Instagram

instagram.com/

Vimeo

vimeo.com/

capnaux

THE MAN BEHIND THE COVER PHOTO
MARK LAWRENCE

Also responsible for the magical cover photos from There I Wuz! Volumes 1 & II, photographer Mark Lawrence is an avgeek that has been around the industry since he was a small child.

An aviation photographer for many years, he is also the Producer for the aviation website NYCAviation.com. He makes his home in Fort Lauderdale, Florida with his wife and son.

Visit Mr. Lawrence's photography Blog at: amateuravphoto.blogspot.com
See Mr. Lawrence's Portfolio at marklawrence.zenfolio.com
email: mark@tavustheman.com.

ABOUT THE COVER PHOTO

Aircraft:
Rockwell B-1B Lancer
Serial number 86-0121
First flight: May 2002
Unit: 37th Bomb
Squadron, Ellsworth Air
Force Base, South
Dakota
Named, "Symphony of
Destruction" in July
2003

Picture taken at the Dubai Air Show, November 2015 shot in RAW using a Nikon D300 and a Nikon 55-300mm telephoto lens, F/8, 1/800s. Edited with Adobe Photoshop CC on an iMac.

ABOUT TEAM AUX
PRODUCER: BUNNY LAVERTY

Team Aux's Producer is Mary Ann "Bunny" Laverty.

A PR guru from the Philippine movie industry, Bunny is responsible for shaping the "product" into the best quality for you. Cap'n Aux may write the stuff, but she polishes it to a shiny perfection to maximize your enjoyment!

She also keeps the boys in line and on schedule.

Bunny also happens to be Cap'n Aux's girlfriend. ;o)

PHOTOGRAPHER: JOHN "OTTO PILOT" KEITH

Team Aux's go-to photographer and videographer is our Tech Supervisor, John "Otto Pilot" Keith.

With us for over two years now, John has faithfully documented many of our adventures, such as Oshkosh, and much of our aerial footage for our videos.

What's more, John's taken the bold step of jumping careers midstream in order to pursue his dream of flying for a living. A private pilot, he is currently working on his instrument rating. Best of luck, John!

ABOUT THE AUTHOR

ERIC "CAP'N AUX" AUXIER

is an airline pilot by day, writer by night, and kid by choice.

Never one to believe in working for a living, his past list of occupations include: Alaska bush pilot, freelance writer, mural artist, and pilot for a Caribbean seaplane operation. He is now a captain for a major U.S. airline.

A Columnist for Airways Magazine, published in over 60 countries worldwide, Mr. Auxier has contributed to such publications as *Plane & Pilot*, *Arizona Highways* and *AOPA Pilot*. *There I Wuz! Volume III* is his seventh book. In 2013, his novel, *The Last Bush Pilots*, captured the coveted Amazon Top 100 Breakthrough Novels Award. He is currently working on two new novels, *Water & Air*, a sequel to *The Last Bush Pilots*, and *Yakuza Dynasty*, Mission 4 of the *Code Name: Dodger* Young Adult, spy/fly thriller series, due Fall 2016.

Mr. Auxier makes his home in Phoenix, Arizona.

NOW BOARDING: VOLUME IV!

MORE...

—Aeronautical
Adventures
—Inflight
Emergencies
—Tough Lessons
—Stories behind
the stories
—Guest
Stories
—Love,
Laughs and
Tears in the
Sky
—Surprises!

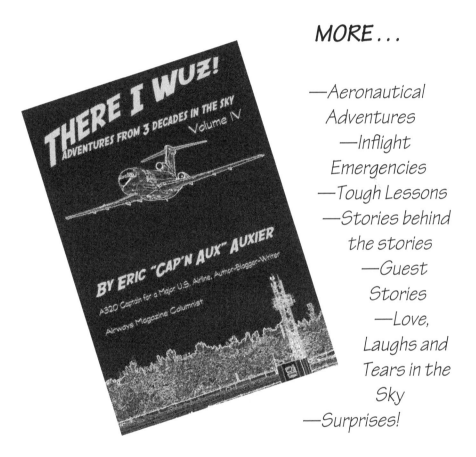

A portion of all author proceeds go to the international orphan relief funds, kinshipunited.org and flyingkites.org

TARGET PUBLICATION DATE: 6/18/17!

Made in the USA
Columbia, SC
29 December 2021

52989461R00098